DERWEN
My World and the Welsh Cob
IFOR LLOYD

DERWEN

My World and the Welsh Cob

IFOR LLOYD

in conversation with

RICHARD MILLER

Gomer

First published in 2018 by GOMER,
Llandysul, Ceredigion SA44 4JL

ISBN 9781785622359

A CIP record for this title is available from the British Library.

This book is published with the financial support of the
Welsh Books Council.

Printed and bound in Wales at
Gomer Press, Llandysul, Ceredigion
www.gomer.co.uk

To my parents, Roscoe and Elin Lloyd,
my wife Myfanwy,
son Dyfed, partner Carly,
and our grandson Rhys.

Contents

Acknowledgements and Credits

Ifor and Myfanwy Lloyd gratefully acknowledge Lyn Ebenezer's contribution to this book.

Thanks also to those who have photographed our animals over the years and have willingly given permission for them to be shared. Many of the photographs are from the family archives. All efforts have been made to trace the owner of the copyright on other pictures. Should you be the copyright holder in any of the images used in this book please contact the publisher.

Jonathan Batt
Johanna Becker
Sian Broderick
Mark Bullen
Bruce Cardwell
Ceri Davies
Dai Davies
Ron Davies
Kenneth Davies
Dr E. Wynne Davies
Gables Studio
Marina Gallery
Carol Gilson

Kit Houghton
Peter Hussey
Charlotte Kelway
Giles Keyte
Hilary Legard
Suzanne Moody
Les Mayall
Trevor Newbrook
Owen Rees-Griffiths
Anthony Reynolds
Dean Smith
Kevin Sparrow

Further reading

I & M Lloyd, **Cobiau Campus Cymru / Winning Welsh Cobs**, Gomer Press 2008
I Lloyd, **Canu, Ceir a Cobs**, Gomer Press, 2014

Links to archive footage
Facebook: https://www.facebook.com/DerwenCobBook/
Youtube: Search for "DerwenCobBook"

Thanks

I was fortunate to be born into a family steeped in the traditions that Wales holds dear.

My grandfather and brother were amongst the founder members of the Welsh Pony and Cob Society at the beginning of the twentieth century.

Following on, my father bought his foundation mare, Dewi Rosina, in 1944.

Encouraged by my mother, I began singing at an early age, and was proud to win the Singer of the Year at the Llangollen International Eisteddfod, together with the Blue Ribbon at the National Eisteddfod of Wales.

In 1964, my father bought Aeron Garage, Aberaeron, for me. I changed the name to Lloyd Motors, and almost a decade later, I became the youngest Volvo dealer in the UK.

I thank you for buying my book, and hope that you will enjoy reading it.

Derwen – an introduction by Richard Miller.

Thirty-six years ago I visited the Derwen Stud on the occasion of their first draft sale of 54 Cobs and Ponies. Seventeen years ago I was commissioned by *Horse & Hound* magazine to pen an article on the Lloyd's successes.

Turning off the road onto the driveway at Ynyshir, in January 2018, on the surface nothing has changed. Everything is still neat and tidy and as you arrive on the yard all is peaceful. It's easy to see that there is a place for everything and everything is in its place. Of course a lot has changed in that time; people, animals, experiences, trends and fashions have changed us all. However the welcome, coupled by an enthusiasm that runs parallel with a duty to the breed and to Welsh culture, is as evident now as it has always been at Derwen.

It was a pleasure to chat with Ifor and Myfanwy to expand upon their last book *Canu, Ceir a Cobs* (Lyn Ebenezer) with the aim of focusing mainly on their Welsh Cob world. The stories, anecdotes and snippets of times past that have led up to Ifor's 2017/18 presidency of the Welsh Pony and Cob Society all paint a picture, each intertwined with the passion the couple obviously have for the Welsh breeds that have been such an important part of their lives.

I decided to play a game with Ifor, without warning. I asked him to name six of the finest people he has known during his life, people that given the opportunity he could welcome back to the kitchen table at Ynyshir to spend some more time together. With little hesitation he came up with this collection of friends, family and associates:

My Father – Roscoe Lloyd

For obvious reasons.

A. L. Williams – Blaentwrch Stud

I knew him since I was a child in Ffarmers, when we lived down the road. He was a gentleman and a top horseman.

Iorwerth Osbourne-Jones – Henblas Stud

He gave me the best piece of advice: 'If you're ever in conversation and you don't know much about the subject, try and get them around to talk about what you do know about without opening your mouth to show your ignorance!'

Emrys Griffith – Revel Stud

He could teach me how to be frugal!

Miss Brodrick – Coed Coch Stud

For her wealth of knowledge in opening up new markets for the Welsh breeds.

Gunn Johansson – Burhults Stud

She has been the greatest friend that Myfanwy and I could ever have, and a trailblazer for the Welsh sections in Sweden.

I was intrigued, then, with all the animals he had known over the years, were there any that he coveted over and above all the rest; that were not in his ownership or bred by him. Again, with little hesitation, he freely offered up the following:

Revel Rosette

I'll always remember the Royal Welsh Show at Margam in 1959 when Emrys Griffiths brought her out in top form. A.L. Williams was the judge. I remember talking to Ronald Jones, the brother of Cerdin, Synod Stud, and he had the same recollection of her too.

Coed Coch Madog

He was one of the loveliest Welsh Mountain Pony stallions ever and my father was one of the first people to make him Champion as a four-year-old.

Bowdler Beggar

'What could have been?'

Gredington Simwnt

He could move for fun and was exactly my type of pony. I can see Dil Powell showing him now at Lampeter, a sight to behold.

Coed Coch Planed

We took a mare, Derwen Delight, to Planed who gave us a wonderful son, Derwen Planed's Delight, who we stood at stud for many years.

Dyoll Starlight

One has to recognise Dyoll Starlight, registration number 4 in the Welsh Stud Book, as probably the most important stallion in the history of the Mountain Pony.

All Mountain ponies. 'No Cobs?' I said. 'Not really. I've got all the Cobs I want.' He replied. Should I have expected a different response? From the man who has owned and bred some of the finest, influential and successful Welsh Cobs in the stud book, probably not.

Perhaps it is that confidence that has kept Ifor, together with Myfanwy, at the forefront of the breed for so many years and will hold them in good standing as we head into the 2020s and beyond. Enjoy the book.

Glossary of Cob Names

Below is a translation of many of the Ponies and Cobs mentioned in the book as well as some prefixes and farm names.

Key:
The phonetic pronunciations include the Welsh double L sound "Ll". It is made by putting your tongue to the roof of your mouth behind your top teeth and blowing.

For the purpose of this guide the "**Ch**" noise is denoted as GH as pronounced in the artist's name Vincent Van Gogh (Goch).

Each name should be said quickly to achieve the desired Welsh sound.

Name	Translation	Pronunciation
Arwr	Hero	*Ah-r-ooo-rr*
Aurwen	Golden smile	*Aye-rr-when*
Bleddyn	Wolf-boy	*Bleth-in*
Bodlon	Contented	*Bod-lonn*
Brenin	King	*Brenn-inn*
Dameg	Parable	*Dam-egg*
Deryn Du	Black Bird	*Dare-inn-dee*
Dewin	Magician	*Deh-win*
Diddordeb	Interest	*Dith-orr-deb*
Dyfodol	Future	*Dove-oh-doll*
Dymuniad	Wish	*Dumb-in-yad*
Enfys	Rainbow	*N-viss*
Golau'r Ganrif	Light of the Century	*Go-lie-r-gan-reeve*
Groten Ddu	Black Girl	*Grot-n-thee*

Groten Goch	Red Girl	*Grot-n-gogh*
Gwenlais	Pure Voice	*Gwen-lice*
Golau Medi	September Light	*Go-lie-Med-ee*
Llwynog	Fox	*Ll-oo-in-ogg*
Llwynog y Garth	The Fox from the Garden Courtyard	*Ll-oo-in-og-ugh-garthe*
Perl	Pearl	*Pear-l*
Rhamant	Romance	*RR-ham-ant*
Rheolwr	Ruler	*RR-hay-oll-oo-rr*
Rhyfeddod	Wonder	*RR-huv-eth-odd*
Seren	Star	*Say-wren*
Serenllys	Starbright	*Say-wren-ll-is*
Seren Ddu	Dark Star	*Say-wren-thee*
Seren Teledu	Television star	*Say-wren-tell-eddie*
Sian	Jane	*Sharne*
Sion	John	*Shorn*
Tawela	The quietest	*Tau-eh-la*
Tegan	Toy	*Teh-gan*
Teithiwr	Traveller	*Tay-th-ee-ooh -r*
Telynores	Harpist (Female)	*Tell-un-oh-ress*
Telynor	Harpist (Male)	*Tell-un-ore*
Tlws	Beautiful Jewel	*Tlooose (as in noose)*
Trysor	Treasure	*Truss-ore*
Ynyshir	Long Island	*Un-iss-heer*
Ynyslas	Fertile Island	*Un-iss-l-ass*
Derwen	Oak Tree	*Dare-when*
Coed Coch	Red Wood	*Coyed-cogh*
Hwylog	Sail-like	*Who-ill-ogg*
Brynymor	The Sea Hill	*Brinn-ugh-more*

Blaenwaun	Before the Moor	*Bl-eye-n-wine*
Coedllys	Court of Trees	*Coyed-ll-eese*
Blaentwrch	Before the Boar	*Bl-eye-n-too-rr-ch*
Cwrt-y-cadno	Fox Court	*Coort-ugh-cadd-no*
Tafarnaubach	Little Taverns	*Tav-are-nigh-bach*

1755   This Prize List is issued subject to the Rules, Orders and Regulations of the Privy Council.   1953

BRECKNOCKSHIRE AGRICULTURAL SOCIETY

*

Coronation Show

Established 1755

Under Special Royal Patronage 1890

SATURDAY
SEPT. 19
1953

OFFICIAL CATALOGUE

PRICE - TWO SHILLINGS and SIXPENCE

*

SHOW GROUND : NEWTON PARK, BRECON

*

Hon. Secretary's Office : 8, SHIP STREET, BRECON.
Telephone : Brecon 103.

"Express & County Times," Printers, Brecon.

Chapter One

The Beginning
'Proceed slowly if you wish to go far.'

The first important milestone on my life's journey was to be born. This event occurred on 27 December, 1943, in a house called Garth Villa, Dre-fach, near Llanybydder, Carmarthenshire, on the road to Llanwenog. However, my stay here was short as my parents soon purchased a farm in nearby Crugybar, some fourteen miles south-east, where we all moved together with my brother Ifan and this could be said was where the foundations of the Derwen Welsh Cob Stud were laid.

My prospective parents were married at Abermeurig Chapel on 14 June, 1928. They joined the Cardi[1] migration to London, settling down at Holland Park in the Kensington and Chelsea district. They bought a milk round, or colloquially a 'milk walk'. They were put up by Aunty Olwen, mam's sister, and her husband, Uncle Dan. The dairy was a corner shop in Islington. They named it 'Aeron Dairy'. They then moved to another corner shop in Chiswick in the Hounslow district of west London.

---

[1] A Cardi is the colloquial name given to someone born in the county of the old Cardiganshire now known as Ceredigion in West Wales

My father would begin his milk round at 4.30 every morning and would do another round in the afternoon. As he made the rounds, Mam would look after the shop.

The milk cart would be drawn by a Welsh Cob. It would take a fortnight to train the horse to work the round, moving on and stopping at every house without having to be urged. This meant that my father could deliver the milk with confidence, without once having to lead the horse from house to house, from street to street. He would start training them for the round at five or six years old. The cob was the perfect horse for such work. It is the most intelligent horse among all the equine breeds. To me it is the greatest breed of horse on God's earth.

Aunty Kitty, Mam's older sister, had also moved to London. Her husband, Uncle Tom, decided early on to take my father to the White City for the Greyhound racing. Every so often he would point out individuals that my father would recognise as having also come up from West Wales, simply adding, 'See him? Gone to the dogs!', and again, 'Him as well, gone to the dogs!' These men had a bit of money come their way, and they'd gone straight to the track to gamble it away. It so scared my father that he never bet a penny on a horse or a dog in his life.

Ifan, who was 12 years older than me, was born in London. My parents had moved there soon almost immediately following their wedding and like so many others from Cardiganshire dreamt of a better and more prosperous life. They saw London not as the land of milk and honey but as the land of milk and money. But unlike most of the London Cardis they did not stay there long; and back they came, bag and baggage to West Wales.

My infancy was not without its turmoil – I was lucky to even see Crugybar. One of my father's closest friends was

Dr Worthington, who lived in Llangeitho. He wasn't our family doctor but he and my father would meet quite often. When I was three years old I was taken ill. There was a large swelling under my chin that resembled a pouch. It was full of puss. Our family doctor at Lampeter didn't seem too worried about it. My parents therefore were rather unperturbed.

One Tuesday evening, following Lampeter Mart, my father was in Troed-y-Rhiw tavern with a few friends when Dr Worthington arrived. Worthington was rumoured to know every pub in the county but as a doctor there was none better. He had served as a doctor on the front line in the Great War and had witnessed some terrible scenes. No doubt that he later suffered from what today is known as post-traumatic stress disorder and found solace in drink. He was much respected by everyone.

My father asked him what he fancied. Worthington would never answer verbally, rather slide two fingers along the bar in the direction of the favoured drink of the day. My father happened to mention my condition and the pouch under my chin. Worthington decided, there and then, to call to see me. My father worried on two counts. For one thing he feared what our own doctors would say to another doctor being involved. Secondly, Worthington had downed quite a few drinks and was neither in a fit state to drive nor to carry out any medical duties.

Worthington would not listen to my father's misgivings. So my father jumped in his car and drove home to Garth Villa and Worthington followed in his own car. Having reached the house, the doctor had to be helped upstairs. I was lying in a wooden crib and I can still remember waking up and seeing this strange man staring at me, a battered old Trilby hat on his head. I can still recall the smell of alcohol on his breath. I believe it was the aroma of the alcohol that sent me back to sleep.

Having examined me he asked Mam whether he could go to the next room to think. He soon returned and seemed as sober as a saint. He made a phone call to the hospital stating that he had a child patient who required immediate attention. Within two hours I was receiving surgery. Worthington had phoned ahead to his wife, who was matron at the hospital, listing his needs.

What no-one but Worthington had realised was that I was on my death bed. Without immediate treatment the pouch under my chin would have burst and the poisonous puss would have entered my bloodstream leading to septicaemia. Doctor Worthington, God bless him, had saved my life.

Garth Villa, in Carmarthenshire, was a smallholding of under 20 acres. The house and outbuildings were fairly new and my parents bought it for £1,250. Blaenwâc, our second holding, was kept on for another four years when my parents bought Y Felin, a holding of some 18 acres bordering Garth Villa. It was shortly afterwards that we moved to Crugybar. There they bought Ynysau Farm, a 104-acre holding that cost £5,000. They also bought Tŷ'n Waun, Caio, a mountain farm of 195 acres.

When we moved we realised that there was a problem. There were no fewer than five farms between the villages of Pumpsaint and Crugybar with the name Ynysau. As well as Ynysau Isaf, our farm itself, there was Ynysau Uchaf, Ynysau Morgans, Ynysau Richards and Ynysau. This meant that letters would often be delivered to any one of the five farms! People calling round would constantly end up at the wrong destination. My parents therefore decided to rename the property. At the entrance there grew a huge oak tree and so they named the farm Derwen Fawr, meaning

Great Oak; which later gave the Derwen Stud its name. Here my parents milked 20 pedigree Friesians as well as running a herd of Hereford cattle as well as Llanwenog sheep.

I have clear childhood memories of Uncle Ben and Aunty Sali of Rhiwseithbren, Gwernogle. We were not related but I regarded them as uncle and aunt. At the time they were childless and virtually adopted me. I would spend my school holidays with them.

I remember once being taken to Carmarthen with Aunty Sali. We were chauffeured by Albert the Blacksmith. My dream back then was to own a Meccano set. She ushered me into a toyshop in King Street. The only set in stock was the smallest version, 'Number 00'. The sets were graded all the way up to 'Number 10'. And Aunty Sali ordered the largest set in the catalogue. Only the best would do. It must have cost her around £20, a small fortune in those days.

It was arranged that the set would be posted on to me. One day as I walked to Crugybar School from our home in Derwen Fawr I spotted Miss Rees, Pen-roc, our local post woman, approaching. Miss Rees would usually be pedalling along, but on this particular morning she was pushing her bike. I soon realised that the reason why she couldn't ride her bike was the size of the parcel she was carrying on the handlebars. I knew immediately that this was my Meccano set and that Miss Rees would have to push the bike for another two miles before reaching Derwen Fawr.

That was the longest school day I had ever spent. The hands of the clock crept round slowly. I imagined the parcel lying on the kitchen table begging to be opened. The Meccano set became a veritable treasure. Indeed, it was more than that; it was educational as well as being a toy. Years later Ben and Sali were belatedly blessed with a son, Aelwyn, and I passed the set on to him as a gift.

At Crugybar there was a geographical divide for the parish, the border running just past our home. The children who lived to the right of the invisible border, on the Llanwrda side, would be taught at Crugybar School. Those to the left would be taught at Caio School. So it was to Crugybar School that I went. The headmaster was Luther Davies and Ray Davies was his deputy. As Ray lived in Ffarmers it meant that she lodged at Crugybar during the week and cycled home to Ffarmers after school on Friday afternoons. We would cycle together until I reached Derwen Fawr and she would continue on to her home, Nantllyn. Ray still lives in Ffarmers and turned 90 in 2017. We still meet from time to time. She was a very dedicated teacher who left no stone unturned in our education. I was lucky to have gained many friends at Crugybar Primary School. Maybe it was due to the fact that at our annual school Christmas party Mam always made a tray full of chocolate eclairs that soon disappeared when they met us greedy children.

When I reached my 11th birthday, the geographical divide also decided which secondary school I would attend. Caio children attended Pantycelyn School at Llandovery, while we at Crugybar went to Llandeilo Grammar School. Those in the area that failed the Eleven Plus attended Llansawel School. I was fortunate enough to pass, so off I went to Llandeilo Grammar. The headteacher here was Mr Samuel and our Welsh teacher was the great poet Mr W. Leslie Richards. Though it was our English teacher, Mr James that was to teach me a valuable lesson. At the outset he said to us, 'Boys and girls, if there's one thing I'm going to teach you, it is how to write a letter.' I have always cherished his advice and wisdom, and in this day of emails and texts it has stood me in good stead. I shall never forget my good friends at Llandeilo: Lyn Griffiths, Howi Davies, Owen James, Gwynfor Morgan but above all, my best friend, David Bowen from Manordeilo.

My first memory of a Welsh Cob was the sight of our very first pony, the Cob that established Derwen Stud. It was Dewi Rosina, bred by J.O. Davies, Pentrebrain, Llanddewi Brefi. She was sold on to a Mr Felix of Llangeitho. One April morning in 1944 my father went to Llanybydder, home of the famous horse sale, held on the last Thursday of every month, though on this occasion he'd gone to buy seeds at Sheffield House, an all-encompassing farmers' cooperative in the town. It was market day, and he was about to set off for home when he heard the clatter of hooves coming from the lane leading to the station. The sound of hooves was music to my father's ears. He couldn't resist the urge to take a look. He saw someone leading an attractive black Cob with a small round roan patch on her rump, the size of your palm, to be sold at the market. He immediately struck a bargain with the owner, agreeing a price of £97 and took her home to Garth Villa.

J.O. Davies, Pentrebrain, Dewi Rosina's breeder, was unjustly criticised by some as being miserly. He would not pay for a service by any stallion from outside his own stud. But this was not being miserly. J.O. Davies' priority was to establish and perpetuate a lineage; and that became our priority as well. In 1951, when I was just eight years old, the Royal Welsh Show was held on the same site as it is today at Llanelwedd although it was, back then, still peripatetic, being held at different locations annually. Judging the horse section was D.O. Morgan, Coedparc. He awarded the George Prince of Wales Trophy, the Blue Ribbon award at the show, to the famous stallion Pentre Eiddwen Comet. As it happened, Dewi

Rosina was Comet's grandmother as well as being his half-sister, his sire Eiddwens Image being her son, and Dewi Black Bess being the dam of Rosina and Comet. We soon appreciated we had to align our own breeding programme with this solid line.

Two years later at Cardiff, with Alfred Williams, Blaentwrch, judging, the order changed. Rosina, then aged 19, won the cup and her grandson Pentre Eiddwen Comet was placed runner up. The judge described Rosina as 'the perfect example of her breed'. It was a wonderful achievement to lift the trophy for the first time; little did we realise at that point that we were to win it another twelve times in the years to come. It was a time of huge excitement for me, aged ten, to see my father winning the Prince of Wales trophy, an experience I shall never forget. I was asked to look after the rosettes, a job I was proud to do, and took very seriously.

Before we moved from Derwen Fawr, Rosina gave birth to nine foals, the last when she was 29 years old. Unfortunately that foal drowned after a brook was accidentally blocked. Tom Jones Evans, of the Welsh Mountain Pony stallion Grove Sprightly fame, offered to pay my father to have Rosina covered by the Champion Hackney stallion, Solitude. Father refused as he remembered my paternal grandfather using a stallion on one particular mare who gave him top stock every time. He became blasé and decided to put another stallion on her to see what she might breed and the resulting foal wasn't as good. Apparently this theory about changing the stallion after a successful repeat mating was outlined in an American book on reproduction, but I don't know if it is true and I can't say that I have followed that logic. So my father reverted to the original stallion but never had as good a foal. Rosina fulfilled the old adage of the working Welsh

Cob better than many; the belief being that a true Welsh Cob would plough the fields during the week, take the farmer hunting on Saturday and the family to church on Sunday.

My father, Roscoe Lloyd, was from Pencarreg, Aberaeron. I am therefore a Cardi from both sides of the family; and yes, the traditions of the concert and the Cob run strongly through that lineage as well. As well as owning Pencarreg, my grandfather Evan Lloyd also owned Blaenau Gwenog, Gors-goch; the Faenog, Dihewyd; Dôl-gwartheg, Aberaeron and Cefn-maes, Mydroilyn. He was born in 1863 and he and his wife Mary had five children.

My father, in his younger days, could sing that old favourite 'Y Marchog' ('The Horseman') as well as anyone. He won first prize singing it at the Aberaeron Cae Sgwâr Eisteddfod with Doctor Caradog Roberts among the adjudicators. Every Christmas Eve a notable eisteddfod would be held at Mydroilyn and my father won the Gold Medal there two years in succession, in 1923 and 1924. He would regularly wear one of them attached proudly to his pocket watch chain strung across his waistcoat. Mam would wear the other on a gold chain around her neck.

My mother Elin was from Pentrefelin near Talsarn, not far from the market town of Lampeter. She was one of the Jenkins family. She was related to the poet Cerngoch. She was born at Llundain Fach, meaning Little London. Appropriately, the brook that runs through the little hamlet is known as the Thames. The Jenkins family were known far beyond the Aeron Valley for their singing and for their cobs well before my parents moved from little London to big London.

Mam, like my father was musically adept. She was a much respected accompanist and was a member of a quartet that held a remarkable record. They had an unbeaten run at 65 eisteddfodau where they were awarded first prize on every occasion.

Why this hamlet of less than a dozen houses was named Llundain Fach has always intrigued me. It may have had something to do with its location on the old drovers' route in the days when those hardy men on foot escorted herds of cattle to the London markets.

Her father Daniel Jenkins married Elizabeth, who lived at Pentre Farm, Llanfair Clydogau. Mam was the youngest of ten children. Daniel studied at Bangor University College and was a schoolmaster for over 40 years. He reputedly had a lovely bass voice. He taught at Cilcennin School in the days of the Welsh Not, when children were punished for speaking Welsh by having a sign hung around their neck stating 'Welsh Not' as in 'No Welsh' and made to face the corner. He, however, insisted that the children be allowed to recite the Lord's Prayer in Welsh every morning before lessons began. But a local family, who were themselves Welsh-speakers reported him to the authorities and he was sacked. An Englishman was appointed to replace him. Yes, Daniel was betrayed by fellow Welshmen. Unfortunately, such things still happen, as I have personally experienced.

Daniel was then appointed to teach at Llanfair Clydogau School earning £60 per annum. At the time a local miller was experiencing problems with a powerful landowner; he could not afford to engage a solicitor so my grandfather acted on his behalf. He won the ensuing court case. As a result of his actions he was sacked again.

It was Daniel who undertook the task of collecting Cerngoch's poetical work in 1904. Cerngoch, his real name being John Jenkins, was Daniel's uncle. At the time there was a school of poets composing in the Aeron Valley. Another uncle of note was Joseph Jenkins, who suddenly left his home at Tregaron in late 1868 for Australia. He became a swagman, wandering around the bush and working on various farms. He led an interesting life working as a gold miner and with a gang of Chinese migrants harvesting corn, before returning to his traditional trade as a farmworker.

Joseph attended various eisteddfodau. At an event at Ballarat in central Victoria he recited a Welsh poem of 22 verses and won first prize. He wandered around Australia for over 30 years before returning home. Ironically the story of this colourful character is better known in Australia than it is in his native land. I sometimes wonder how proud he would have been that, a century later, I would sell a Welsh Cob stallion Derwen Serenllys to tread the same soil in Australia.

When my parents left London in 1935 with my brother Ifan, who was then just two years old, they returned to farm Faenog Isaf, Dihewid. They were there for three years. They also owned Blaenwâc, a 60-acre farm. They sold it in 1942 for £1,050. But for some years after leaving London my father would send Welsh Cobs to milk vendors both in the English capital and to Birmingham. They would be transported by train from Llanybydder station, around half a dozen at a time according to the vendors' requirements. It is difficult to compare the value of today's money with its worth towards the end of the thirties, but it is possible to estimate roughly how they compare. One day my father called with Mr James of Morfa Mawr Farm, Llanon, to settle a deal for a mare. Morfa Mawr was a 600-acre holding and was one of the best farms in the county. As they discussed the price of the mare, Mr James surprisingly offered the farm together with all the animals and machinery to him for a total cost of £3,000. This would equate to £1.4m in today's money.

In 1938 there was a horse in the village of Llanarth called Llethi Valiant, owned by the Richards family. It had won at the Royal Agricultural Society of England Show held that year in Cardiff. There were buyers there from Australia and one of them offered £5,000 for the horse but he was refused. This turned out to be a blessing for us in Wales as Llethi Valiant contributed greatly to the breed.

My preoccupation in breeding, buying and selling these awesome beasts is not surprising seeing that I struck my first bargain when I was only five years old. It did not involve a Cob but rather a dog. I went on holiday to Y Dyffryn, Dihewid, to the home of my cousin Eryl Pugh's parents. Their neighbours at nearby Saron owned a Jack Russell bitch. I wanted it and haggled for it, settling for two shillings. My mother named it Two Bob. Thank goodness that I didn't have to pay sixpence more or it would have been named Half Crown!

It was obvious that buying and selling was in the blood. Later as a youth at Crugybar I met up with two brothers, members of the Emanuel family, who collected sacks from local farmers which was in essence an early recycling service. The Emanuel brothers would pay two shillings a sack; and like Baldrick's character from *Blackadder*, I had a 'cunning plan'. I offered to collect the sacks on their behalf and store them at Derwen Fawr. This would save them the trouble of travelling to collect them. They agreed, paying me a percentage for every sack. As it was my father who paid for the Land Rover's diesel used to collect them it was a profitable scam for me. On Saturday nights I was able to go out with a wad of notes in my wallet. I was flush!

My exile from Cardiganshire did not last for very long. Derwen Fawr and nearby Tŷ'n Waun were sold for a total of £33,000 in 1962. We moved back to Aberaeron from Carmarthenshire on the advice of Mam's doctor as they felt the sea air off Cardigan Bay would be better for her health, purchasing Ynyshir between Aberarth and Pennant where we remain today. My father was of course coming home. They bought our new business at Compton House, a hardware store. Aberaeron, being a Georgian port town, has the central Cae Sgwar (Square Field) as its focal point. Compton House sits in a prime position on the corner of the square.

When we left Derwen Fawr I was still studying at Gelli Aur and Pibwrlwyd Colleges in Llandeilo and Carmarthen. I then left my studies to work at Compton House as an apprentice. In 1965 my father bought another business, Aeron Garage, for £10,400 and Ynyslas, another farm adjoining our home at Ynyshir. At one time both had been a single unit, and so we re-united them.

Following the sale of Compton House, my father bought Falrona Farm at Felinfach where Aunty Kitty, mother's sister and her husband Uncle Tom lived. He also bought 100 acres of Esgairarth. Buying and selling was part of our family's DNA. At one time my paternal grandfather, Evan Lloyd, owned five farms!

In the meantime my mother's family continued farming Pentrefelin. There is an interesting story involving Jack Jenkins, mother's brother. Around the time of the outbreak of the Second World War, a few days before the Talsarn Races, a lady called at Pentrefelin, a complete stranger. She asked Jack whether he would let her borrow a horse to race at the meeting. She sounded Irish and was tall and shapely and seemed rather wild. Jack let her borrow a young pony, Spitfire, that was, true to its name, rather sprightly. At the races the stranger riding Spitfire won their race. It was only later that Jack realised that the woman was Caitlyn, Dylan Thomas' wife, who was staying at nearby Gelli Mansion. Dylan was working in London scripting propaganda war films and would join his wife at Gelli at the weekends where he would often be seen at the local pub, the Red Lion. Pentrefelin, where Mam's family still farm, is central to the family history. It is also pivotal to the establishment and development of the Derwen Stud. Before my parents married, my father had called to see my mother at Pentrefelin. He also met his future father in law. He was busy packing various volumes of *The Welsh Pony and Cob Stud Book*; of course it was the cob breeders' bible. Since none of his sons were interested in keeping them, Dan Jenkins had intended sending the whole collection to the National Library of Wales at Aberystwyth for safekeeping. But when he realised that my father was keenly interested in the stud books he gave them to him. They are still with us and not a single day passes when I don't turn to them for information.

It has to be said that I'm a great believer in fate, a trait I inherited from Mam. If it's meant to be, so be it. I am also superstitious – for example I will never leave a building through a different door than the one I entered. I remember years ago my grandmother always painted the doors to the farm buildings in red, except for this one time she decided to paint them green. The following day the whole lot burnt down! If it's a tried and tested formula stick to your guns.

In fact it was Mam who turned me into an autograph hunter. She would collect all kinds of memorabilia, newspaper and magazine cuttings. She would never discard anything.

The Llanwnen pack of hounds meet at the crossroads near Neuadd Fawr, Hafod, Nantcwnlle, Carmarthenshire.
Mr and Mrs Hughes, Neuadd Fawr, Dafydd Davies, Talfan, the Whip. My father on his Welsh Cob (Bess of Pentrefelin by Welsh Model out of Betty by Cardi III) - Dan Jenkins, Pentrefelin. The father of Capt Hex-Lewes, Llanllyr standing.

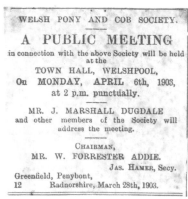

WELSH PONY AND COB SOCIETY.

A PUBLIC MEETING

in connection with the above Society will be held at the
TOWN HALL, WELSHPOOL,
On MONDAY, APRIL 6th, 1903,
at 2 p.m. punctually.

MR. J. MARSHALL DUGDALE
and other members of the Society will address the meeting.

CHAIRMAN,
MR. W. FORRESTER ADDIE.

JAS. HAMER, Secy.
Greenfield, Penybont,
12   Radnorshire, March 28th, 1903.

My Aunt Caroline, fathers sister, on her Cob, "Violet", taken at Pencarreg, Aberaeron.

My mother, Elin Lloyd, in 1968 with Derwen Groten Ddu and right, my father E.Roscoe Lloyd, founder of the Derwen Stud.

Blaenau Gwennog farm workers in 1910. One of five
farms owned by my grandfather, Ifan Lloyd.

Garth Villa, my birthplace in 1943.

ROYAL WELSH CARDIFF 1953

From the left: "Jack" Hughes, (owner of Pentre Eiddwen Comet), Roscoe
& Elin Lloyd, Mrs. Davies and Iowerth Osbourne-Jones (Henblas) at the
1953 Royal Welsh Show.

Dewi Rosina.

The Family farm, Derwen Fawr, Crugybar, Carmarthenshire.

Aged 18, at Derwen Fawr with one of our original
Mountain Ponies, Bowdler Banger by Criban Pilot.

1961, my first time in the ring at the Royal Welsh Show with Coedllys Stardust.

My father and I with Derwen Rosina and the Prince of Wales Trophy 1966.

1966 Royal Welsh Show with Derwen Rosina.

Singer of the Year, Llangollen, 1971.   My marriage to Myfanwy 1974.

Lloyd Motors, Aberaeron.

Mam instigated correspondence between myself and Sir David Attenborough when I was very young which resulted in an autograph. I had seen him on television with an African tribe that practised intermarriage in the belief that it would keep the tribe as a strong unit. In the world of horses my father sought perfection through linebreeding. This ensured, of course, that he was able to retain the best breeding virtues within the stock. It is not as simple as it sounds. You must always be very aware of the animals' lineage.

Among all the autographs signed by celebrities, my most cherished signature is that of Mr R.E. Isaac, the surgeon who operated on me at Aberystwyth Hospital by removing my appendix. Under his name he wrote *'Festina Lente'* meaning 'Proceed slowly if you wish to go far'.

Another treasure is my Aunty Olive's autograph. Yes, my lovely Aunty Olive who for years kept the books in good order at the garage in Aberaeron. She wrote, 'Home is the place where you grumble the most and are treated the best.' Poring over my autograph collection still evokes sweet memories.

During this period we were joined as a family by Richard Schubert, who was a German prisoner of war who came to work for my parents when they farmed at Drefach, from the camp at Henllan, near Llandysul.

Richard stayed with them as a trusted and faithful servant for 34 years, moving with them to Derwen Fawr and then on to Ynyshir. He hailed from East Germany and had no intention of returning after the war ended. Although he was a butcher by trade he had a great affinity with animals and really became my father's right hand man, handling and breaking in all manner of horses. One day, back in 1952, we had a telegram from a Mr Gaskell wanting to buy Derwen Sian to go to France, on the condition she was broken to drive in the next two weeks. Richard took it upon himself to get the job done and sure enough she was soon hooked up to the old gambo, the farm cart. Richard took some slats out of the floor of the two wheeled vehicle, so he could easily jump in and out. Sian made it to France after a fortnight's training much to the delight of all concerned. Richard sadly passed away in 1980 and is buried in Henfynyw Church alongside my parents.

My childhood and early youth were days of innocence. This was the era that formed my character; the years that made me what I am. Every neighbourhood has at least one person who is inspirational, someone who encourages young people to contribute socially by being involved in various activities. In our neighbourhood, that person was Mam. She was my first singing coach. I well remember my first-ever competitive success as a soloist. It was at a small eisteddfod at Cwrt-y-cadno near Llanwrda. I was six years old.

One of the stalwarts of the district, socially, was the Rev. Glenville Rees. There were others such as Rev. Idris Evans in Llanllwni and Rev. Giraldus Morgan in Ffald-y-brenin. The highlight of the year would be the *Cwrdd Cystadleuol* – a competitive meeting between the local chapels. The rivalry would be fervent. For many of us, this would be our first competitive platform. But even more than the singing, what really gave me confidence was the impromptu address competition. This gave me the self-reliance to face an audience, without fear; something I have profited from over the years.

As a family we did not have any problems in settling in our new locality, be that in Crugybar, Aberaeron or Pennant. As they had done earlier in London, my parents immediately became a part of the community. They easily conformed and did not seek to push themselves in any way; it was a gradual integration and that's how it should be in any community.

Moving from one area to another can also cause problems. The worst aspect is leaving old friends and settling among strangers and not knowing what awaits you. But when our family moved from Crugybar to Aberaeron and then to Pennant we were immediately embraced by the local community. In a way I was going home to Aberaeron as I had been living for some time with Uncle Henry and Aunty Mari at the Feathers Hotel which looks directly over the Square Field. When Myfanwy and I got married, my parents moved to Ynyslas and we took over Ynyshir, where we still live.

We had family in the area before we moved, Ifan, Roderick and Griff, Wern-ddu. I must refer to Aunty Peggy as she was known to everyone in the neighbourhood. She kept the Ship Inn at Pennant and was a real character. The relationship between her family and ours went back centuries. Peggy had milked cows for over 40 years so when the creamery lorry appeared for the last time to collect the churns that were being phased out, she bedecked them each in black ribbons, flowers and epitaphs to mourn their passing, much to the bemusement of the driver. Peggy, along with many small farmers, gave up milking when the churns were done away with.

Going back to Aberaeron and my father's propensity to deal, he was always keen to diversify. After he'd bought the hardware shop, Compton House, in 1963 he bought Aeron Garage, next door to the Feathers Hotel for £10,400 and renamed it Lloyd's Motors.

The actual garage building was of a zinc sheet construction and the price my father paid for it included a car that still remained there. It had the registration AC1, the two letters notifying that it had been registered in Coventry. Today that number would be worth a fortune. But the man who sold the garage secretly sold the car without informing my father.

I had spent two years studying agriculture at Gelli Aur and a year studying mechanics at Pibwrlwyd, though I left to become an apprentice in the hardware shop. When I began the mechanics course I had no inkling that my father would be buying a garage. But as fate would have it, that course was now a godsend. I had already obtained my certificates in agriculture and mechanics, meaning I was already qualified to inspect cars, including MOT tests.

Having lived on a farm I could drive any kind of vehicle from a very early age so as soon as I reached my seventeenth birthday I applied for my test. I was so eager that I asked to be tested only a few days following my birthday in 1961. A neighbour and a good friend of mine, Esme, had passed her test at the first attempt and if she could do it then I felt that all I needed doing was to turn up. It would be a doddle.

My father accompanied me to Lampeter for my test. He emphasised that I should stay calm and to use my head. He offered to hang around to keep an eye on me. But no, I felt I was fine. I can still see the tester. He wore a trilby hat and had a moustache. I duly filled the official form in the office and off we went.

A friend of mine who had taken his test at Lampeter had forewarned me to expect an emergency stop in New Street. He said that the tester would suddenly slap the dashboard with his hand and shout 'Stop!' and I was ready for it. From the corner of my eye I saw the tester looking slyly at me. He raised his hand. But before he could slap the dashboard and shout 'Stop!' I hit the break. Sharply! There were no safety belts in those days, of course, and the tester was very lucky not to be hurled through the windscreen. I had forgotten my father's advice to relax and to use my head.

Back we went back to the testing centre. My father was there waiting for me. The tester and my father embraced each other. They were close friends having been together in school but hadn't met for some years. 'Roscoe!' exclaimed the tester. 'Is this your son?' 'Yes,' said my father, 'I hope you've passed him.' 'Unfortunately not,' he replied, 'I've already filled in the form. He broke a few rules. He broke the speed limit going through Cwmann. He made a mistake while turning and he almost killed me with his emergency stop!'

Yes, I came down with quite a bump. But I did learn from it. I learnt not to take anything for granted. There was another lesson to be learnt as well – my father knew better than me. On reflection today I have a feeling that the setback I suffered then was more good than bad for me. Fortunately I passed my driving test just before my father bought the garage in Aberaeron. I admit that it did not deter me from making many other mistakes. Before making my way home from work I would often call for a drink in town at the Royal Oak with Mr and Mrs Davies. Their granddaughter, Heather runs The New Celtic Restaurant at Aberaeron. Behind the Royal Oak pub were old stable buildings that had stood empty for many years. One night over drinks we discussed the possibility of growing mushrooms there. The magic word of the time was diversification. The dark old stables were perfect for such a venture. Layers of rotting horse manure still covered the floors. I ordered mushroom spawn. We couldn't fail.

Mr Davies and I then sowed the spawn. Nothing grew. Not even one mushroom.

Later Mr Davies decided to have the stables cleared. A local farmer from Ffos-y-ffin called to do the work. He removed the soil and horse manure and dumped the lot on his dung-heap. Within a few weeks he had a crop of thousands of mushrooms. The heat from the dung heap had helped the spawn germinate! Yes, another harsh lesson.

I was only 19 years old when I started at the garage. My duties at first involved selling batteries and tyres; and I learnt a valuable lesson right at the very beginning, a lesson I never forgot. One day a man called in a white Bedford van that looked as if it had seen better days. The driver looked more like a scrap metal dealer than a delivery man. He wore a muffler round his neck and hadn't shaved for some time. He needed a set of tyres, '550 x 12'. He asked me for a price and I gave him a quote for £16.

We agreed on the price plus the cost of changing the tyres and he left while the job was being seen to. He seemed to be a suspicious character and I shared my feelings with Gwilym, the senior mechanic. What if he returned and refused to settle the full price? After all, he didn't seem to be someone who could afford to pay even a comparatively small amount of money.

He returned and checked the tyres and asked me to remind him of the cost. When I did, he shook his head and complained that the price was too high. It was just as I had suspected. I stuck to my price and he took a wad of notes from his pocket. It must have amounted to some £2,000. He peeled off the amount he needed and passed the notes to me and away he drove. I was told later that this man, who was indeed a scrap merchant and who lived near New Quay, Cardiganshire, was one of the richest businessmen in the county. That day I learnt the meaning of that old adage that includes the words 'book' and 'cover.'

It was through the car business that Myfanwy and I met. One disadvantage of running a business in Aberaeron was it was literally one-sided. We had the sea cutting us off on one side. I heard that Morris Isaacs' garage in Llandovery was on the market, a well-known business situated adjacent to the railway crossing. The owner, Mrs Hancock was ageing and felt it was the right time to sell. At the time Morris Isaacs' held the franchise for Ferguson tractors in the area.

I drove down to Llandovery and met up with Mrs Hancock and the others involved. I happened to look towards the office and one girl drew my attention immediately. The garage discussions came to nothing but as I drove home I kept thinking of the pretty girl I had seen in the office. I knew nothing about her, not even her name.

I turned to my old friend Daniel Evans of Cefngornoeth for some assistance. Daniel's family were customers at Morris Isaacs' garage. He kindly offered to play detective by tracking down the girl from the office.

Daniel not only identified her but also discovered her phone number. I took the plunge and phoned, asking her if she would show me around Llandovery. What a chat-up line! What I hadn't realised was that Myfanwy had also made enquiries to Mrs Hancock about me and, best of all, that the good lady had kindly given me an excellent reference.

Our first date was not a very romantic affair. I took her to a meeting of the West Wales Pony Breeders Society at Carmarthen. The society was set up by Emrys Bowen, Tom Roberts and I at Carmarthen. Myfanwy had little interest in horses. Her family, who lived at Pantywheel, close to Llandovery, kept sheep as well as a milking herd

She and I, however, shared a common interest. Her father was musically inclined and was a member of the Llandovery Male Voice Choir. He was also a member of the South Wales Choir and had, with my future mother-in-law, travelled with them worldwide.

Fortunately everything developed from that first date at the Pony Breeders Society meeting. Things went smoothly but with a few bumps along the road. Somebody told her father that they had seen me with Myfanwy driving rather perilously. I was supposed to have taken the bend past the West End Café at Llandovery on two wheels. That didn't go down well at all.

We began dating in 1972 and were married two years later. It wasn't therefore a long affair. I knew from the very beginning that she was the one for me. I knew that I didn't have to look any further for a wife. Some tend to linger before taking the plunge. I decided however to strike while the iron was hot. Or in equine parlance, while the horseshoe was hot.

There is an old tradition in Wales of mischief-making on the eve of a wedding, especially country weddings. Ours was no exception. On the eve of our wedding the wedding cars were all polished and lined up ready inside the garage at Aberaeron. The white ribbons had been festooned around the doors and bonnet. But by morning all the doors had been chained and padlocked and it took some time to break the chains and release the cars. There was worse to come at my parents' home at Ynyslas, where I had spent the night, dozens of straw bales had been built-up across the doors blocking our exit.

The bridesmaids were Sheila, who was Myfanwy's friend

from their schooldays, and Lilian, one of her cousins, Glenys, my second cousin, and Llinos, my niece.

The ceremony was conducted by the Rev. Elwyn Pryse, a wonderful character. It was a day to remember and a day to treasure. Gerald Davies sang 'Panis Angelicus' during the service.

It was no secret that marrying Myfanwy also meant marrying a wonderful cook. But even the best suffer off-days. Soon after we were married we welcomed some visitors. Naturally, we invited them round the table. Myfanwy had baked some cakes, and as I ate one I asked her what kind of cakes they were. She described them as rock cakes. I couldn't resist adding,

'Unfortunately, more rock than cake!'

Wisely she never again baked rock cakes, though luckily she has perfected a fine Lemon Drizzle cake that is a particular favourite at our regular 11 o'clock coffee break.

Myfanwy has three brothers. Vivian and his wife Ann still farm the old homestead at Pantywheel. They have a daughter, Anwen. Huw and his wife Carol keep an electrical goods shop at Llandovery. They have three daughters, Catrin, Sara and Megan. Carwyn, the youngest brother, is now a minister at Tregaron, having ministered at Treorci in the Rhondda. His wife, Alisia, is from Patagonia and when she came over she had no English, only Welsh and Spanish. She is by now tri-lingual.

Working at the garage, cars became an increasingly important part of my life. The changeover to a Volvo dealership was not an easy one – it being a Swedish product and the tendency amongst the local car-owners to favour the traditional British brands.

I received my first Volvo in 1971. I exhibited it proudly but no one wanted to know. I would offer test drives to my regular customers but once they realised it was a Volvo, that would be that.

I finally managed to break through thanks to a vet who regularly visited my parents' farm. Ifan Williams, Pennant, was an old family friend. One evening as I returned from the garage he was there sipping tea with my parents. After some discussion I managed to sell him a Volvo. Vets are renowned for their hard driving. They are asked to travel along rough tracks very often and as a result they have to change their cars more often than most, so the use he gave the car became a good advertisement, although his choice of a white-coloured model perhaps wasn't the most practical. His partner Tom Herbert then changed to a Volvo and subsequently so did our Member of Parliament, Lord Geraint of Ponterwyd. The rest is history.

As the Volvo cars made inroads to the customer base we looked to expand the business.

My next venture was to buy the Seabank Garage at Llanrhystud in 1978. The previous owner was known to all as Captain Pugwash. Attached to the garage was a restaurant, which we developed and rebranded as 'The Welsh Cob'. It was roomy enough for meetings and dinners. Indeed, we staged a few cabaret-style concerts there.

Our next step was to buy the old Lowndes Garage on North Parade, Aberystwyth, with repair facilities based at Llanbadarn Fawr. Nelson's Garage in the town had closed, leaving a gap in the car repair business. We also the bought The Old Foundry Garage at Cardigan with its workshop located across the river Teifi. The workshop, however, we sold to J.J. Morris, the local auctioneers who wanted to expand the mart site. We now owned four garages in the county, employing over 70 staff at one time.

Volvo sales in the meantime grew, as did the cars' reputation. I have been asked many times whether there is a special gift in buying and selling. There is, but I don't believe it is a gift that one can ever learn. The most important aspect is for the salesman to have sufficient self-confidence in his product. Without that, there is no use in attempting to persuade anyone to buy. With Volvos, I had that confidence. Any fool can lie about what he sells. The penalty is that the buyer will not return to be made a fool of a second time. The best advert of all was the fact that I myself drove a Volvo 144. It was yellow with black stripes adorning the sides – it made me feel that I was a real Jack the Lad!

Like the singing, the car business led to making friends throughout Wales. One of the most famous was the artist Kyffin Williams. I have a barrister friend in Neath, James Jenkins. We would meet once a year to talk about old times. In 1991 he happened to mention Kyffin. Back then he was only a name to me. But realising how good an artist he was, I told James that I would like to commission him to paint a portrait of the finest Welsh Cob I owned at the time, Derwen Replica.

He said that I shouldn't just pick up the phone and talk to a man like Kyffin. But having downed a drink or two I decided to prove that I could. I knew he lived on Anglesey and that he drove a Volvo. This I knew through Tŷ'n Lôn Garage, who were themselves Volvo dealers and were friends of mine. Kyffin was a neighbour and friend who bought and serviced his cars through them.

I rang Kyffin. He immediately agreed to come down to paint Replica. Having got to know him I would visit Kyffin every six months or so and I would drive him around the area at his direction showing me the sights. He was an islander from head to toe. He knew every inch of Anglesey. Much later I took the portrait to the BBC's *Antiques Roadshow* when it visited Aberystwyth. I was told that it was worth a considerable sum of money.

When our son Dyfed celebrated his 18th birthday Myfanwy and I commissioned Kyffin to paint him a picture. It portrays a shepherd and his sheepdog, one of Kyffin's favourite subjects.

During the time when I was concentrating on Volvos, my centre of operations in Pembrokeshire was at Hendrewen Farm, the home of Idris and Cynthia James at Manorowen, near Fishguard. I would call there twice or three times a week. Cynthia was known for her charity work, forever organising fundraising events. I remember her asking me whether I could arrange for Trebor Edwards to perform in one of her events. I did, and Trebor became a close friend of the James'. When Cynthia died a few years ago, Trebor was at her funeral.

Another Pembrokeshire family I became friendly with through the Volvo connection were the Cornocks. Joy Cornock is a very successful soloist and Georgina Cornock-Evans was the Royal Welsh Lady Ambassador for 2017, having married into the Eglwysfach Stud, near Ffarmers, but my connections with the family go back to her grandparents. Once again we have the cars, concerts and Cobs as a link.

Even after I gave up the garage business, Myfanwy and I still had connections with the trade until fairly recently as my brother Ifan and his daughter Llinos continued in the business at Aberaeron. When I came out of the business in 1985 was when I turned to breeding and selling Welsh Cobs. As I shipped Cobs out to Europe and Scandinavia and in Swedish ports especially, I would see thousands of Volvos awaiting transit to Britain. This would always rekindle old memories.

One day I received a telephone call from Geraint Rees, director of the weekly programme *Cefn Gwlad (Countryside)*, shown weekly on S4C, the Welsh Channel 4. He invited me to replace Glynog Davies as the presenter. I gladly accepted and fronted a series of programmes. One of my most memorable programmes was one with Dan Theophilus, his forefathers being from Greece. One of his exploits was stilt-walking. We filmed him doing so while crossing the river Tywi. Dan lived at Cil-y-cwm, above Llandovery, and when he was younger he would cycle all the way to the Cross Inn sports meeting, some 30 miles away; compete successfully and cycle 30 miles home. This was all on an old fashioned pushbike. He was quite a character.

Another programme that I well remember is one I filmed with the Owens family from the Friars Stud at Star on Anglesey. The Owens are a remarkable family. Both the daughters, Ann and Sian, are dentists while their brother Gareth is a doctor. Their parents bred mountain ponies and as we filmed on the yard behind the house, one of the ponies decided to gallop away down the road. I jumped into Mr Owens' car and he drove after the pony. What I didn't realise was that Mr Owens was an ex-police car driver. That's the fastest I've ever been driven. It was like being on *The Sweeney*.

Filming could be most interesting. Every day would be different. We once filmed a woman who kept a calf in her kitchen. I spent a day out hunting. I even took part in a programme on ferreting. The work was so varied.

We filmed closer to home at Frongoy near Pennant, home of the famous Fronarth Welsh Cob stud. We also filmed farmer and singer Trebor Edwards. I spent almost two years with the *Cefn Gwlad* crew, a most enjoyable experience.

I occasionally filmed with vet Huw Geraint for the series *Mil o Alwadau (A Thousand Calls)* again screened on S4C. One programme showed the birth of a foal seldom caught on camera. I also presented programmes from the Royal Welsh Show, but gradually, as the responsibility of running the business rested more and more on my shoulders I had to give up the television work. *Cefn Gwlad* was taken over by Dai Jones who presents it to this day.

Some of our Derwen cobs have become television stars. In 1981 the BBC would send presenter Hywel Gwynfryn to different parts of the country. One centre he called at was the Felinfach Theatre. I received a call asking whether I would be willing to take one of our Cobs over there. I decided to take the chestnut stallion Derwen Replica.

It was November, with the nights drawing in. I was asked to bring Replica in through a rather narrow entrance at the back of the theatre while Hywel addressed the audience. He was to face the audience pretending he didn't know that Replica and I were behind him. Hywel pretended to bemoan the fact that there were no Cobs left in the county. In pantomime fashion he shouted,

'There are no Cobs!'

The children in the audience countered with, 'Oh, yes there are!'

Then Hywel again, 'Oh, no there aren't!'

And Replica, as if performing to the producer's cue, stepped forward and, with his nose, poked Hywel in the shoulder. It was perfect timing!

We were also invited down to the BBC studios in London to appear on *What's My Line?* Once again Replica appeared in the studio. Angela Rippon was the presenter and the panel members were footballer Garth Crooks, the author Jilly Cooper and comedian Roy Hudd. I was the last competitor to appear and I was introduced to the audience without my profession being revealed, as was the custom, but disclosed to the audience and viewers as a Cob breeder. I needed the panel, after the maximum of ten questions, to fail to discover my profession. But after eight questions, Jilly Cooper came up with the correct answer. Replica was then led into the studio where he stood in front of the cameras like a seasoned television performer, and once again, on cue, he pawed the floor with one hoof. Perfect!

Chapter Two

Breeding
'You have to be focused.'

Some maintain that the Cob came to Wales with the Romans. Others believe it to have evolved from the Mountain Pony. It is a debate that hasn't ever been resolved. But I have a feeling, albeit with no historical backing, that the Cob has been roaming the Welsh hills for thousands of years looking for his ancestral home and he ultimately found it among the Cardiganshire hills.

Some time after Myfanwy and I were married she returned to Derwen Fawr and collected a fistful of acorns from under the great oak by its entrance and planted them here at Ynyshir. Two acorns took root and two oaks are now growing proudly. Acorns can be harmful to horses but the two oaks symbolise to me what I've always attempted to do with my cobs – establish a succession. The perpetuation of the oaks symbolises the continuation of the Derwen Cobs. 'The strength of a tree is in its roots and not its branches.'

The key word in breeding Cobs and Ponies is lineage. It applies not only to the horses but also to those who breed them, and I am proud to be able to boast that I am from a long,

31

rich horse-breeding ancestry. Both my grandfathers were Cob breeders and exhibitors. My maternal grandfather, Dan Jenkins, and his brother who lived at Pentrefelin, Talsarn in the Aeron Valley were breeders and were among those who founded the Welsh Cob and Ponies Society in 1901. Sarnicol, a local poet and writer, described Dan thus:

'Tall, robust and commensurate; a brindled beard, wide forehead and cheeks like August apples; a pair of blue eyes with a peasant-like modesty under his eyelids. A concoction of the teacher, the preacher and the farmer's attitudes; that is Dan Jenkins, Llan-y-crwys - a Cardi among the very best.'

Evan Lloyd, my paternal grandfather, bred Welsh Cobs although no prefix was recorded at the time. He also kept the popular Hackney stallion Thornton Chandos as well as the Champion Shire, Bonnie Royal Harold, whose trophies we still have here at home in the cabinet. Ironic then that my first Horse of the Year Show judging appointment was the Ridden Heavy Horses. My parents inherited the tradition, and along with it the skill to buy and sell to keep the stud business in profit, something they passed on to me.

My first foray as it were into linebreeding was to study Ancona chickens, a breed originating from Italy with black mottled feathering. Facing our farm, Derwen Fawr, was the home of Griff Davies. Griff was known as the Ancona King. He began breeding Anconas with two hens and a cockerel that he was given as a child and bred scores of birds during his 50 years of breeding. His birds twice won the British Championship for Any Breed. Very much in character with Cob breeders, Griff bred his birds from within his original stock without introducing any alien birds. He then bought a bird that had been a part of his stock originally from the Vicar of Caio thus perpetuating the breed. We have always entwined the blood of our foundation mare Dewi Rosina through our Cobs.

At the highpoint of breeding and dealing in Cobs we would have close to 60 mares and followers and maybe eight stallions at Derwen, which we felt were needed for us to continue with our serious programme of linebreeding. Today we have closer to 30 animals on the 130-acre holding above Cardigan Bay.

Handling and riding Cobs has been second nature to me from my beginning. Yes, I have often been unseated but considering all those thousands of horses I have handled over the years I consider myself lucky. One explanation for this has been the fact that we have bred Cobs from one mare. She was docile and her offspring have all inherited that same quality. That is why bloodline is so important.

When we still farmed at Drefach my father bought a two-year-old colt from John Berry of Betws-y-Coed. His son is Gwyn Berry who still runs the Betws Stud. My father travelled up to see the colt with his old friend Iorwerth Osborne-Jones, Ystrad Meurig. Our family and the Osborne-Jones' were very close friends. I used to spend holidays at their home, Henblas, playing with the youngest son, Raymond.

My greatest thrill would be to see the train steaming along the railway line that crossed the Henblas fields. The line between Aberystwyth and Carmarthen was open back then. Lord Beeching's axe put paid to it in 1963. Later Raymond was the founder of the popular magazine *The Welsh Cob Review*, writing under the pseudonym Sherlock Jones. Most readers believed Sherlock Jones to be a real person but it was Raymond in disguise.

My father struck a deal with John Berry and he followed

him and Iorwerth down as far as the Cross Foxes near Brithdir, Dolgellau. There, as they parted, hands were spat upon and clasped, the traditional way of sealing a bargain. The new colt was named Llwynog y Garth and when the Cross Foxes was reopened by Dewi and Nicole Gwynn recently I called there and presented them with a photograph of the Cob and it now hangs in the bar.

Father sold Llwynog y Garth at Llandeilo show at the beginning of the fifties to Dil Thomas from Neath. He became very successful both in hand and in harness. My father once again proved to be canny in such matters. Many years later I realised that we needed to re-introduce the blood of Llwynog y Garth so I decided to source the stock from the tremendous mare, Tireinon Spring Song, who had been to Derwen several times visiting our stallions, Derwen Railway Express and Derwen Replica, so her stock incorporated the blood of Dewi Rosina. Spring Song was by Hendy Brenin and out of Cathedine Pride, a daughter of the Llwynog y Garth son Cathedine Flyer.To secure the Llwynog y Garth bloodline her daughter Tireinon Gwenlais, and son Tireinon Step On, both by Railway Express, joined us at Derwen but I also asked Roy Higgins, Tireinon, that if he could secure the remaining full brother, Tireinon Confidence, would he let me know. I waited patiently and sure enough Roy eventually phoned one day to say that David Wray who owned Confidence in the north of England had decided to sell. Straight away I went to pick Roy up and we headed north. We phoned David from the M6 who was quite taken aback when Roy said we would be with him in 30 minutes but we weren't going to miss this chance. A deal was done and 'Herbie', as he was known, was secured for £15,000 though I only had £10 on me to give David to secure the deal. A man of his word, the following day he refused a bigger offer for him to go to

America, saying, 'I only sell a horse once!' These three Tireinon descendants were joined by their Replica half-brother Tireinon High Noon from the Cathael Stud and between them they have been a welcome and successful addition to the gene pool here.

Almost 50 years have passed since I struck my first successful bargain. I bought that first Cob at the Hwylog Stud at New Cross near Aberystwyth. It was November 1970 when Mr & Mrs Rowlands were running the stud before the present owners, Richard and Buddug took over. The horse was Hwylog Sensation and it was, apparently, Pentre Eiddwen Comet's last foal to be born.

When I took it home, my father and Richard the farm hand were rather scornful. They were only pulling my leg, of course, although I didn't appreciate it at the time. I sold Hwylog Sensation to Bunny Doyle, Swyddffynnon, and he went on to win the championship at Talybont show as a two-year-old. He was then sold to a stud in France having enjoyed many show successes over the years. Bunny made the unique oak horseshoe fireplace that sits in our lounge from a design that can be seen to this day on the right hand side of the A487, above the old forge door as you enter Machynlleth from Aberystwyth.

Back in 1964 my father went to Lampeter Stallion Show and noticed a nice black two-year-old colt who was standing fifth in his class. He didn't have a catalogue and nobody else seemed interested in how this colt had done so that was that. Later on, a gentleman from Cilcennin who people referred to as 'Bridport', whose wife used to teach father to sing, had called into Compton House and just casually asked him if he wanted to buy a good colt. Always on the lookout for a good colt father was told 'There's a good one available at Lluest-hen, with Geraint and Mary Jones.' So after shutting up the shop, he travelled that night to have a look. Geraint proudly brought the colt out and father immediately recognised him as the one that he'd seen and liked at the show. He bought him for £294. His name was Nebo Black Magic. The following year he won the prestigious Robleith Cup at Lampeter Stallion Show. A while later Eddie Price of the Regency Stud from Marlow in Buckinghamshire, who had previously bought several animals from us, happened to be on the yard. He asked how much Magic was. Father replied that he wasn't for sale but Eddie prompted him to put a price on the animal if he were ever to be sold. Father thought, 'I'll block him now and say a high price of £400,' and Eddie said right away, 'Fine, I'll have him.' Father was so disappointed, it was the worst thing he'd ever done but he wouldn't go back on his word.

We would always have the catalogue for Llanybydder sale and years later there he was – Magic; entered for next month's sale. So father said to my mother, 'Come on, we're going to buy him back.' But Magic never turned up at Llanybydder. Not to be deterred my father packed his bags and went off to London only to find him in a pig farm! He stayed with Uncle Ifan and Aunty Bet in Middlesex and were told that Magic was on this farm in Essex. They bought him and then found out he was due to be slaughtered the next week as the then owners weren't interested in the horse. Nobody knew how he'd got there. He was transported back to Derwen in an open top truck, not a proper livestock carrier, which of course gave the problem then as to how to unload him. There being no ramp. Not to be outdone, Richard, the farm hand suggested we reverse the lorry up to the muck heap, he climbed up into the lorry and spoke to Magic who seemed to recognise Richard's voice from his early years and together the two walked out onto the muck and eventually hit Welsh soil once again.

What transpired as a result of his return was that a Mr Taylor, Denham Stud, made a complaint to the Welsh Pony and Cob Society that the Magic that had returned from Essex was not the same Magic that had left Wales, which caused a lot of upset and ill feeling but thankfully following blood-typing techniques he was proved to be wrong. Not content with this he then made the accusation that the stallions Derwen Llwynog and Derwen Rosina's Last were not full brothers, so they were both blood-typed and were proven correct which of course they were, so as they say, the rest is history.

Black Magic was Prince of Wales Cup winner in 1973 as well as champion at the Royal of England qualifying for the Wembley In-hand Championship of the year at the Horse of the Year show, sponsored in those days by Lloyds Bank. He returned to the Royal Welsh in 1975 and was male champion. He certainly left his mark for us and indeed the breed. Everything father bought in for the stud had to be related to Dewi Rosina, a plan that was tried and tested time and again.

One day back in 1962 my father called to see Mr Evan Williams, Rhandir Uchaf, Llangwyryfon, and as he looked around the Cobs a black filly grazing on a nearby field caught his eye. He and Williams struck a bargain and he bought her for £45 and named her Derwen Rosina as in those days a purchaser could add their own prefix. This one again harked back to the original Dewi Rosina and became very successful. She won us the Challenge Cup three times in succession at the Royal Welsh, in 1966, 1967 and 1968. She was covered as a two-year-old by Llanarth Braint, purely to ensure that she would foal at the right time for the show the following year, a plan that paid off. The result was Derwen Deryn Du who became a stud stallion at the Amos family's Redwood Stud in Aberaeron for all his life. My father turned down a bid of £5,000 for Rosina from Hugh Edwards, Sarnau Park. Unfortunately we lost her to what we now realise was milk fever. She was only eight years old, leaving us to raise her colt, Rosina's Last, with the help of a foster mare. Thankfully we did as Rosina's Last was top of the sire ratings in 1976 and tied with his sire in 1978, and our stud would be a poorer place without his influence.

Derwen Rosina again was a daughter to Cahn Dafydd, who in turn was by Mathrafal. Rosina gave birth to Derwen Queen and Derwen Seren Teledu. The latter was given her name because there was a television crew with us at the time. In 1967 a television company were making a film about Cardiganshire and wanted to film Cobs so John Hughes brought Pentre Eiddwen Comet up to Ynyshir from Llanrhystud to be filmed alongside Derwen Rosina. As it turned out, the mare was horsing so before he left, she was covered and that produced Derwen Seren Teledu, the Welsh for 'Television Star'! Normally of course we would have travelled the mares to him.

One of her sons, Derwen Telynor was sold to Nelson Smith and was the founding stallion at his Trevallion Stud in Coventry. Queen was the only other filly I can recall that we covered as a two-year-old and she had Princess, so that again dispels the myth that first foals can be write-offs.

Father used Hendy Brenin on Derwen Rosina to produce Derwen Queen who was the foundation of what we refer to as the 'Royal' line. We sent the mare down to Idris Davies in Usk. At that time there were only really five devotees that thought anything of Hendy Brenin: Roy Higgins, Tireinon, John Thomas, Gwendraeth, Cerdin Jones, Synod, my father and Dennis Bushby,

Buckswood. People used to call him a cart horse, but he was a beautiful horse.

The resultant foal from this mating, Derwen Princess, won the Prince of Wales Cup twice at the Royal Welsh and three times at the Royal of England. Her half-sister, born three years later, Derwen Viscountess by Rosina's Last, also won the Prince of Wales trophy in 1985 for the Haak's Uplands Stud from Hampshire. That year, when Princess was a foal at foot, was the only time we showed Queen. Mostyn Isaac was judging at the Royal Welsh and he pulled her in fifth place. After her individual she had given such a tremendous show, fair play to the man, he pulled her up to win the class!

Another purchase from Llanybydder sales was Groten Ddu born at Croesasgwrn, Llangyndeyrn in the Gwendraeth Valley. She was big for a mare. The old couple living at Croesagwrn had died and the mare had been sold on. She couldn't get in foal as she was too large; in fact she was obese. As a result my father bought her for just £45. On her return to Derwen from the sale she was put out to graze on the moor at another of our holdings, Tŷ'n Waun at Caio.

Groten Ddu rapidly lost weight in her new environment. My father then decided to take her to John Hughes, Rhydlas' Pentre Eiddwen Comet. She was transported in Dai Davies, Y Felin, Llansawel's lorry one Sunday night. John, however, refused to co-operate. He was determined to observe Sunday as a day of rest. We had to hang on until one minute past midnight on the Monday morning before the mating could take place! Groten Ddu eventually had an influence here as the dam of Derwen Groten Ddu, who was by a tremendous horse, Teify Valiant Comet. He was one of the fastest trotting Cobs I've ever run with. Mated to Derwen Llwynog, Derwen Groten Ddu produced Derwen Groten

Goch. The original Groten Ddu was by Hercws Welsh Comet and out of Polly of Hercws, and we registered the prefix Hercws in Myfanwy's name to protect it from future unworthy use. We then went on to win the Triple Crown of the Cob world with Derwen Groten Goch three times within six years, in 1986, 1990 and 1992. She was by Derwen Llwynog. The 1986 judge commented, 'I have never judged a mare that could move better.'

Father was invited to judge the Welsh Cobs at the Royal Welsh Show in 1974, but he was taken ill. So, at the last minute they called me in to deputise. I selected Brynymor Welsh Magic, or 'Magic Bach' as we came to know him, as Junior Champion and Reserve Male Champion. Now if I'd had the knowledge and confidence that I have now, I would have put him to win the Prince of Wales trophy that day, even though he was only a yearling at the time. We heard after the show that his breeder, Mr D J Thomas, would consider selling him. So my father and I went up to Talybont to see him. Mr Thomas told us that he had several people asking about him, 'but as you were the one to put him up, then if you want him, he's yours'. In those days there was often a case when a judge would put a good animal down the line and then get a friend to go and buy him cheaply afterwards. We bought him but a short while later, Peter Grey, Thorneyside, persuaded me to part with him. That 'persuasion' involved a lot of money and a good home so the decision was made. We had his full sister in Brynymor Aurwen so the blood wasn't lost and, as it's turned out, it has given us tremendous satisfaction to see him and his offspring flourish at Thorneyside. I suppose there is a small hint of regret, it would be foolish not to feel it, but as it happens we may now have our own 'Magic Bach' returned to us in the shape of Derwen Dusk (Derwen To The Quartzite x Derwen Dania by

Derwen Quartz). This stallion goes back to the original Dewi Rosina 29 times in his pedigree.

We showed Dusk to win at the Ceredigion Foal Show before he was sold to Maria Borvall in Sweden. She had a lot of success with him, being a very good horsewoman herself, but at four years of age she sent him away to be broken to drive. What happened to him there, Lord only knows, as when he returned he was extremely nervous.

In the meantime we had sold Maria several mares, including Derwen Tegi (Derwen Requiem x Derwen Tegan by Cefn Parc Boy), on the understanding we would have a filly back at some point, by Dusk. Well when Dusk returned home it was apparent that he wasn't going to be happy in the surroundings there, which like many properties in Sweden was predominantly paddocks made up from electric fencing, so we changed our agreement and Maria kept the foal out of Tegi and Dusk returned to Ceredigion. Turned out with his mares, overlooking the sea; he's been as good as gold ever since, repaying us in 2017 with a lovely filly foal, Derwen Twilight out of the Tegi daughter, Derwen Tess by Derwen Trumpeteer. Twilight has four crosses of Derwen Llwynog and 20 crosses back to Dewi Rosina and as a foal has won three firsts and a championship. Like my mother, I'm a great believer in fate.

Another horse of great notoriety closely connected with Derwen was Mathrafal, bred by Meyrick Jones of Meifod in Powys. He had been sold to Gwil Evans, Dyfrdwy, who farmed with his father at Llangollen. Father and son brought Mathrafal to Llanybydder sale and among the prospective buyers were Ifor Richards from the Vale of Glamorgan and his cousin, Dil Thomas. It became a bidding war between them and another bidder and they went up to £83 before Dil conceded. But Ifor persisted, raising the bid by £1 and he won.

Ifor Richards farmed at Treos on the outskirts of Cowbridge and, soon after buying Mathrafal, he sold a substantial parcel of his land to the Ford Company who built their factory there. In 1952 he had been successful at the Royal Welsh held at Caernarfon when Gwilym Morris, Brecon, judged the Welsh Cobs. Born in 1936 Mathrafal was later sold to Cardiganshire as an old horse to the Fronarth Stud.

I would often call to see Ifor at Treos on my way home from filming or visiting south-east Wales. In 1976 I contacted him asking whether he still had any progeny of Mathrafal. He said that he knew of a horse at Coedtrehen between Port Talbot and the Rhondda. He had been ridden to hounds but hadn't been used at stud.The horse was a 24-year-old stallion, Cefn Parc Boy.

I had to go to a meeting in Brecon so I took the trailer with me.I travelled down and found the old stallion tethered to a post in gypsy fashion in an old shed. Following some intense haggling where meat man prices were mentioned, I managed to buy him for £110. This does not seem like a lot of money but his age at 24 was against him. He could easily have proven infertile. He was mated to Derwen Telynores but it didn't seem as if the mating had been successful. I recalled my father's advice years earlier. He was a firm believer in Doctor Green, his way of describing grassland. The stallion was turned out to pasture and he later sired nine foals. His influence on the stud still remains. He remained fit and well right to the end, clearing a five bar gate out of the yard at 25 years old! Among his descendants was Derwen Dameg, the mare that won us the Prince of Wales Cup at the Royal Welsh in 1989. I remember the lady that judged to Horse of the Year Show qualifier that day pulled me in eighth position in the line-up. Dameg went out in her individual show and flew around with her tail up and we were pulled up to Reserve. A great moment.

In 1981 we enjoyed our sixth Challenge Cup success with Derwen Rosinda, a daughter to Nebo Black Magic and Derwen Seren. Rosinda became the only Derwen mare to appear on the cover of the *Horse & Hound* magazine.

In 1983, and the following year in 1984, Derwen Princess was awarded the Challenge Cup twice in succession. Once again this filly was descended from Nebo Black Magic and Derwen Queen.

Meanwhile, during all these successes, Derwen Dameg, by old Cefn Parc Boy and out of Derwen Duchess, won the championship at the Royal Welsh and the Royal of England during the same year. This made the grand total of 13 Royal Welsh championships in all, quite a feat.

At the 2015 autumn sale of Cobs I bought back Derwen Golau'r Ganrif (Derwen Prince Charming x Tireinon Gwenlais). I always remembered her as a tremendous mover as a foal and being by Prince Charming (Derwen Replica x Derwen Princess) she could be a valuable addition as we hadn't many of his offspring left due to his being away in Holland for so many years. However I knew she hadn't been the best of breeders for her previous owner, so Gwyn Frongoy suggested I took her to Richard Thomas from Talgrwn Veterinary Services, near Lampeter. Although he wasn't our vet, his father had been many years ago when we lived in Crugybar when I was a child. Unfortunately, despite everybody's best efforts, she still remained empty but I asked Richard if it would be alright just to run her with the stallion and he couldn't see any reason why not. Luck was on our side and Derwen Sea Adventure caught her right at the end of the season and we've been rewarded with a lovely filly, Derwen Golau Medi who is an unbelievable mover. She doesn't set off unless she puts her tail over her back! So, after eight years of the mare not breeding, my gamble in giving her the chance to come home has paid off and we hope to cover her with Dusk in the future. Myfanwy says she knew I was going to buy her back without even discussing it!

Another mare to return home was Derwen Diddordeb by Tireinon Step On and out of Derwen Dania who was herself a granddaughter of Derwen Dameg. Diddordeb had initially been sold as a foal for 850gns at our sale in 2008. She was entered in the autumn Cob sale in 2012 as the third lot in on the Sunday morning, so I said to Myfanwy we'll do something we never do, and we went up the night before to make sure we were there in plenty of time so as not to miss her. I got her for 500gns! The maiden bid. There was nobody else up in time to see her go through the ring! I was delighted. We have plans now for her to go to Derwen Quartzite, who I think is one of the best we've bred.

Quartzite is out of a mare called Derwen To The Future, whom I saw being born at 5.30a.m. Before I had returned to the house she was named. Little did I know then that she would be influential here as dam of the stallion Quartzite and grand-dam of Dusk.

Winning prizes is always very pleasing, as is a good sale, but I have to say nothing comes close to the excitement of witnessing when the foals are born, especially if it seems like it's a very good one. We tend to name them within the first 24 hours of life, having generally left the mares until they are four-year-olds before their first mating as I'm adamant that it's worth the wait, giving them time to mature both physically and mentally.

Generally foals' names start with the first letter of their dam's name, with the exception of the 'Royal' line. Stallions run with the mares from mid-May to the end of June, so the foals arrive with the season's grass. We rarely tend to wean the foals before five months of age and they are stabled, whereas the mares winter outside with access to a big barn and big bale hay.

Knowing which ones to keep and which to sell is always a challenge, but having the confidence and knowledge to act when the opportunity to purchase an individual you have previously bred and sold is sometimes a gut feeling.

Buying back Derwen Llwynog in the mid-seventies was one of the most important decisions made for the stud. My father hired him out to Mrs Beaumont from Scotland to run out with thoroughbred mares. Mrs Beaumont was an aunt to the lead singer of the rock band Fleetwood Mac. She then moved back to Wales to live near Crickhowell and eventually in 1974 entered him for the Llanarth sale where we were able to buy him back for 760gns to become one of the most influential stallions we've ever had. Llwynog was among the first registered Welsh Cobs to complete the 50-mile Golden Horseshoe Long Distance ride across Exmoor, and to think at one point Mrs Beaumont had considered gelding him! His part-bred son 'Hansel' met up with him at Ynyshir in 1985 during his 3,000-mile trek around the UK raising money for Age Concern. Partnered by Geoff Gough, the pair averaged 20 miles a day.

A stud is built on the success of its bloodlines but is also helped along the way by its support team. Just as a good blacksmith is important for the show ring, a good vet is for the stud farm, one you can depend on, such as Ifan Williams and Tom Herbert. I should refer to another in particular, although he wasn't local. Rhisiart ap Owen was a partner at the Fyrnwy Veterinary Surgery at Llanymynech, near Shrewsbury. He had studied in Canada but returned to Wales so that his children could be brought up in Welsh. Rhisiart has saved many a horse for us and I would go as far as to claim that I have never met a more knowledgeable man in the treatment of horses. One of his great attributes was that he concentrated on treating horses, and only horses. He was an equine expert.

A stud has births and deaths as with all breeding enterprises. I am often asked which of our Derwen cobs has been my favourite. It was undoubtedly Replica. Unfortunately we lost him when he was only 16 years old. But his influence remains and, strangely, is getting ever stronger. Our good friend **Carol** Derrick wrote this poem for us after his passing;

For Replica
He was a dream horse,
a sire supreme,
a gentle character.
a friend

His passing, a heartbreak,
a nightmare unforgiving;
an untimely end.

His spirit, a soaring shining light;
a song,
a requiem.

His legacy,
a treasure house;
a store of dreams to come.

Derwen Rosina by Cahn Dafydd, out of Rhandir Black by Pentre
Eiddwen Comet, Prince of Wales Cup winner 1966, 67 & 68.

Roscoe & Derwen Rosina.

The Prince of Wales Cup, first
awarded in 1908.

Mathrafal, foaled 1936, photographed here when he won the Prince of Wales Cup in 1952 at Caernarfon with his owner, Ifor Richards (in jacket) and Dilwyn Thomas.

Eiddwen's Image, foaled in 1940, by Mathrafal Eiddwen out of Dewi Rosina.

Cefn Parc Boy, by Mathrafal, photographed as a two year old in 1954 at Margam Show with Howell Richards, son of Ifor Richards.

Llwynog -y-Garth, by Mathrafal, foaled in
1944, purchased by my father in 1946.

Pentre Eiddwen Comet with John Hughes. Foaled in 1946, bred by
J. O Davies, Pentre Brain. Out of the same dam as Dewi Rosina,
the mare Dewi Black Bess F.S.2 by Ceitho Welsh Comet.

My first pony, "Snowflake", purchased in 1947.

Loading Derwen Fair Lady, a daughter of Criban Leading Lady, and Derwen Countess at Llandovery Railway Station on their way to Belgium, circa 1960.

My father with Clan Dash at the 1962 Royal Welsh Show in Wrexham.

Nebo Black Magic, Prince
of Wales Cup winner, 1973.

Derwen Rosinda, foaled 1970, Prince of Wales Cup winner 1981 but
above all else the dam of Derwen Replica by Derwen Llwynog.

Replica and myself representing
the breed at the Parade of Stallions,
Ermelo, The Netherlands, 1984.

The watercolour painting of
Replica by Sir Kyffin Williams.

Brynymor Welsh Magic on the yard at Derwen during "Cob Week".

Derwen Llwynog at home ridden by Alison Smith and
his daughter Derwen Rosa ridden by our son Dyfed.

Derwen Llwynog
at home 1985.

His son Derwen Rapport, sold
to France and then bought back
before being exported to Sweden.

Hendy Brenin with his owner, Idris Davies, Porthvaynor Stud.

Derwen Queen, daughter of Hendy Brenin, winning
at the Royal Welsh as a three year old.

Derwen Princess, daughter of Derwen Queen, by Nebo Black Magic,
Royal Welsh Champion 1983 & 1984.

Derwen Dameg, grand-daughter of Queen, by Cefn Parc Boy, Prince of Wales
Cup winner 1989, pictured here being Champion at the Royal of England.

Derwen Viscountess as a yearling winning at Lampeter
and then winning the Prince of Wales Cup in 1985.

Being presented to her Majesty The Queen in 1983 on the occasion of Derwen Princess's championship, accompanied by Lord Geraint Howells of Ponterwyd.

Derwen Dameg in fine form at the Royal Welsh in 1989.

Derwen Rosina's Last and myself. Never shown but leaving us an incredible legacy.

Derwen Dymuniad by Rosina's Last out of Derwen Duchess, went on to be one of the foundation mares for the London Stud.

His son Derwen Rebound prior to his flight to the USA in 1976.

Derwen Last's Request, Llanarth sale topping filly foal in 1976 by Rosina's Last.

Derwen Rosina's Last captured by Maggie Steel from a photograph by Idris Aeron.

Derwen Telynores, as a three year old, by Rosina's Last, out of Derwen Seren Teledu a daughter of Derwen Rosina. Aberystwyth Show 1976, judge Colin Davies, Cefn.

Telynores, as a mare with Myfanwy, being Champion at Cothi Bridge Show.

Derwen King Last, by Rosina's Last out of Derwen Queen. Top of our 1981 Draft Sale at 1,900gns.

Rosina's Last's Royal Welsh winning progeny group 1976. Left to right - myself with Derwen Viscountess, Roger Hendy with Derwen Nest and John Hendy with Derwen Supreme.

Rex the Sheepdog.

Cwta, the Manx cat.

Replica had everything, the height, the stance and the perfect head. When he was taken sick we took him to Rhisiart ap Owen at Llanymynech. He was suffering with a strain of botulism. It is often caused by something present in silage. It affects horses but is harmless to cattle. This was in 1994 and there was no antidote in stock for treating him. We did manage to fly in a consignment from America but it was too late. We lost him far too soon. Rhisiart ap Owen diagnosed that it was botulism that killed him, although we'd never fed silage nor even haylage. The puzzle was uncovered a few years later by a Belgian veterinary student who was here, who asked us if there was a shooting estate nearby that was raising pheasants. They had lost three horses in Belgium due to botulism that had occurred as dead birds had unknowingly been baled up and infected the food source. We do of course have a shoot next door so maybe that was the answer. Replica's influence is such that he appears four times on one of our present cobs, Derwen Reason's passport. Reason is now seven years old. Through her Replica lives on and his characteristics can be seen on his great-granddaughter, a white star on its forehead, for instance, although Reason has four white socks while Replica had only two white socks on his rear fetlocks.

It was Myfanwy who named Reason. The mother in this instance is named Rhyfeddod, meaning Wonder and so her foals' names must begin with the letter 'R'. When this filly foal was born I told Myfanwy that this, probably, was the best we had ever bred. Her answer was, 'That's the reason why we are here.' And thus was she named Derwen Reason.

As for Ifan Williams, or Ifan the Vet as he was known, he retired some ten years ago but he has been succeeded by his son, Eifion. Ifan could treat any animal; and as for Tom Herbert, I would need a separate book to do him justice by relating some of his exploits. Tom was absolutely unique.

I worry, however, regarding the state of veterinary surgery today. For one thing the qualification requirements are set very high. A future vet needs three Level 'A' Star grades before qualifying for a veterinary college and there is a distinct scarcity of young men among those in training who come to us for experience. In fact they are almost all girls. Treating a horse that is experiencing birth problems, for example, can be a physically taxing, especially for a young girl. I would estimate some 80% of veterinary students today are girls.

Girls, in every educational field, tend to do better than boys. But there are exceptions. A few years ago a young lad from this area was intent on becoming a vet. Dyfrig Williams had a special gift in dealing with animals. He was accepted at the Liverpool Veterinary College. He is now a partner in a veterinary practice in Denbigh. But he is an exception. I'm afraid today that he is in the minority.

Breeding has its extreme highs and desperate lows. Just a few months before foaling in 1989 I could see Derwen Dameg was uncomfortable, pawing the ground. She wasn't that far away from her due date, but I knew instinctively that something was wrong. I called to Myfanwy to telephone Rhisiart ap Owen to tell him that I was on my way. I had to leave Dameg at his clinic near Shrewsbury and he later told me that he'd identified that the colic was caused by a piece of infected intestine. He operated to remove the problem and in doing so had to remove and then replace the foal! Incredibly both mare and foal recovered well and Dameg foaled naturally without problems soon afterwards at the clinic so we decided to call the foal Derwen Distant Adventure. We were in a tizz then as to what to do, as she was entered for both the Royal Welsh and the Royal of England, but we gambled and she was Champion at both. That was a true circle of highs, lows and highs for the stud.

Lately we have felt that we were running low on the blood of Derwen Prince Charming so Gunn Johansson kindly offered to lease us his son, Derwen Gladstone, who is out of Tireinon Gwenlais. He returned to Ynyshir for the month of May 2017 in order to cover some mares. He travelled over with his own groom who cares for him at home in Sweden, Elin. She took time off from her job as a police detective and together with her husband and children, Johan, Lisa and Linnea spent the month in the cottage here having a holiday and looking after Gladstone.

We have never really sold colts by auction unless it was the occasion of our own sale, relying on our reputation that people would buy privately. In the early days of the Llanarth sale at Blaenwern we only sold fillies on the open market, so it is satisfying to be able to list the influential sires that were born in our fields:

Derwen Welsh Comet (foaled 1947 by Cahn Dafydd x Dewi Rosina) was sold to Pakistan through the British Export Agency.

Teify Valiant Comet, bred by J. H. Davies (foaled 1960 by Pentre Eiddwen Comet x Teify Welsh Maid) to Eddie Price, Regency Stud, Marlow, Buckinghamshire after he'd left us Derwen Groten Ddu, the dam of Derwen Groten Goch.

Derwen Black Magic (foaled 1966 by Nebo Black Magic x Derwen Rosie) went to Dyfed's godfather Gareth Evans of the Hewid Stud and then when he was older he travelled to the Bucklesham Stud of Peter and Diana Ravenshear in Suffolk, leaving such good winning Cobs as Bucklesham Prince Arthur.

Derwen Dewin (foaled 1970 by Nebo Black Magic x Derwen Rosie) who stood at the Ross Stud of Malcolm and Charmian Richards.

Derwen Telynor (foaled 1972 by Nebo Black Magic x Derwen Seren Teledu) was purchased by Nelson Smith of the Trevallion Stud near Coventry as a yearling. He had originally planned to purchase Nebo Black Magic from us but when I told him he wasn't for sale he purchased Telynor. The 2017 Prince of Wales Cup winner was Trevallion Rossana who has a double cross of Telynor and was shown by Nelson's grandson Dean.

Derwen Supreme (foaled 1975 by Derwen Rosina's Last x Derwen Seren) remained in our ownership most of his life but had spells at the Sydenham Stud, possibly as he was a grandson of Coedllys Stardust, then at the Tuscani Stud. He had a successful ridden showing career with the Judge family and eventually was purchased by Suzanne Alexander-Ford of the Tor-y-Mynydd Stud. He sired the winning progeny group at the Royal Welsh Show in 1992.

Derwen Railway Express (foaled 1978 by Nebo Black Magic x Derwen Rosie) went to the Batt family, Abergavenny Stud, as an older horse as by that time we had the Tireinon-bred sons of his as well as enough offspring.

Derwen Red Marvel (foaled 1978 by Nebo Black Magic x Hafael

Rosina). Owned by Hilary Legard and George Coombes, he became a Hunter Improvement Society Life Approved Non Thoroughbred stallion and produced some superb part-bred animals. He also appeared in the 1984 Olympia Horse Show Musical Ride that featured Cobs jumping through hoops of fire.

Derwen Desert Express (foaled 1982 by Derwen Railway Express x Derwen Duchess) to the Llewellyn brothers, Tredegar, who leased him initially to the Ty'r Eos Stud of Rob and Val Robinson and then the Lloyd Family, Geler Stud. The brothers came to buy a filly, but we'd sold all the fillies so I showed them this nice colt and the rest is history. Desert is, of course, the sire of Crugybar Mabon Mai who was such an influential sire bred by my good friend John Williams who accompanied me to my first day at Crugybar Primary school all those years ago.

Derwen Paddington Express (foaled 1982 by Derwen Railway Express x Derwen Princess) to David Smith's Broughton Stud in Aylesbury, Buckinghamshire, who had recently become a member of the Welsh Pony and Cob Society in 1981 although he was continuing his father's stud that was founded in 1963.

Derwen Dairy Express to Milton Jones, Min-y-Ffordd (foaled 1984 by Derwen Railway Express x Derwen Duchess).

Derwen Royal Express (foaled 1986 by Derwen Railway Express x Derwen Duchess) went to Roy Davies, Tregare, who was another of Dyfeds' godparents. He also had the chestnut **Derwen Trysor** (foaled 1976 by Derwen Llwynog x Derwen

Seren Teledu). Royal Express came back for a season and we still have one mare by him.

Derwen Timekeeper (foaled 1988 by Derwen Replica x Derwen Tlws) exported to Finland.

Derwen Prince Charming (foaled 1985 by Derwen Replica x Derwen Princess) went to Eddie de Vin in Holland but returned to Derwen.

In the same vein we are proud that the females have established studs worldwide. However the most notable must be Derwen Viscountess. We sold her when she was a three-year-old to the Haaks of the Uplands Stud on the occasion of their silver wedding anniversary. It has always been said that nobody in Cardiganshire would sell anything good enough to come back to Wales and beat the Welshman for the Prince of Wales Trophy. However Dan Haak managed to travel up from Hampshire to do just that when Viscountess was a five-year-old, with a foal by Derwen Disturbance at her side, under William Harris, Pennal Stud, who judged the Royal Welsh that year. The foal at foot was named Uplands Empress and she eventually made her way to Canada. That day in 1985 saw Replica and I stand reserve, 30 years after the only other stud ever to have bred both the Champion and Reserve, Meiarth King Flyer and Meiarth Welsh Maid back in 1954.

My biggest regret to this day is losing Derwen Replica at just 16 years old.

Replica's influence is getting stronger here each year. The filly foals we have retained this year, Twilight and Golau Medi, have strong infusions of his blood. This was another reason why I bought Golau'r Ganrif back from Kevin Hopkins of the Lidgett Stud because she was a Replica granddaughter. Losing Derwen Rosina at such a young age was such a shock but at least she had left us both Llwynog and Rosina's Last to carry on the line. Buying back Llwynog was a pivotal decision for the stud which made him a very influential horse, not only for us, but for other people. For instance he sired Ifor Evans' Pantanamlwg Red Fox, winner of the Prince of Wales Cup in 1991 when Ifor, at 72 years old, ran right round the main ring with him. Another Llwynog Royal Welsh winner was Mark Swistun's Osbourn Rosette in 1996.

I'll always remember Tom Evans, Cathedine, saying to me about Llwynog, 'Just to think that horse was just down the road from me (in Crickhowell) and I never used him!'

Sometimes today it appears that the younger generation never realises that we had so many Welsh Mountain Ponies through our hands over the years. I remember going to the Hay-on-Wye sale some years ago and George Preece of the Bowdler Stud had a pen full of mares he was selling, straight off the hill, mostly grey, long manes and long ears but amongst them, standing in the middle of them was a sweet little bay. She was beautiful and I thought to myself, 'I'll have this one cheap now.' Mr Evans, Tan Lan, from Anglesey was sat by the side of the ring and I was behind the auctioneer and she cost me 460gns which today, 35 years on, was a tremendous amount of money. She was Bowdler Bussy by Bowdler Ballistite. Quality will always out though, in the same way I remember my father buying Revel Tiptoe in the early sixties from Emrys Griffiths, the Revel, for £400 and in the end he had to mither Emrys for some 'luck money' in return and eventually, after two hours, got threepence back as Emrys told him you have

DERWEN · MY WORLD AND THE WELSH COB ❧ IFOR LLOYD

all the luck you need in the pony! We were however treated to lovely homemade cakes that his wife Dinah had baked.

'Tom Fardrefawr' was Myfanwy's uncle, and he was a keen breeder, studying lines and so forth in a way that is missing these days by so many. There are now more Verdrefawr mares with Gunn at Burhults in Sweden than are left with Tom's grandson Robert who still farms near Carreg Cennen, Llandeilo.

We'd always had Mountain Ponies around the place as long as I can remember, as many as 50 at one time. We had a very famous bay mare called Criban Leading Lady who was a granddaughter of the legendary Criban Socks, the mare that was the model for the Welsh Pony and Cob Society logo and car sticker. My father bought her from W.J. Jones, Cellan, and at some point she had had a broken leg but it had healed leaving only a scar. Her most famous daughter was Derwen Delight, also a bay, foaled in 1959 by Bolgoed Revelation. When I finished in the car business in 1984 we cut back to about 25 Mountain Ponies but then we had to decide whether to concentrate on the A's or the Cobs as it would have been too complicated to do both properly with A stallions and Cob stallions and so forth. Most that we kept were grey. When I judged the Section As at the Royal Welsh in 1987 after the first class my steward, Robert Thomas, turned to me and said, 'There you are, then, and you'd better go home now as we know exactly the type you want us to pull in!' Usually I find the type of pony I like is grey.

When I buy a Mountain Pony, and I've bought hundreds over the years for export and so forth, I have to imagine a child sitting on them. The criteria I look for are a long front, good tail set, neat bone, and of course a tidy head.

Back in the sixties we had some success with Clan Dash

who father had purchased from Emrys Griffiths along with the mare Clan Heather. Emrys had bought all the Clan ponies from Mr McNaught after his death. Dash went to Lord Kenyon at Gredington only to find his way to the Aquila Stud in America. We had a mare called Derwen Dot, who was by Clan Gylen, that we happened to be showing under Mr McNaught in Pembrokeshire County Show where she won, much to his surprise. Clan Gylen was by Criban Pledge out of a Coed Coch Glyndwr mare and was at one time owned by the Williams family at Rhandir Uchaf and we borrowed him from them for a couple of seasons. He was a lovely pony. I remember going to Capt. and Mrs Brierley's home at Daywell Manor with my father to buy Brierwood Honeyway who was later exported to Denmark.

I came home from the Coed Coch dispersal sale in 1978 with three ponies but missed out on my fourth wish as I was the under bidder to Mrs Gadsden, Bengad, on Coed Coch Saled. You can so easily get carried away on an occasion like that and he sold for 14,000gns. The seven-year-old mare Coed Coch Bodlon, the dam of Coed Coch Bleddyn and the two year old fillies, Coed Coch Ruthene and Coed Coch Rhamant, headed back to Ceredigion. Whilst looking at the Coed Coch ponies in the paddocks before the sale I always remember going to one field of mares and overhearing a couple discussing, 'These are far better than those youngsters in the last field' and the other one said, 'Yes, but you have to remember these mares were once those youngsters.' They couldn't see, they didn't know. Miss Brodrick was another exponent of linebreeding and what isn't always appreciated by the younger generation was that Miss Brodrick and Emrys Griffiths, The Revel, were not only great friends but they used blood from each other's studs. They were brilliant breeders, there's aren't so many good breeders around these days.

I remember going to George Preece, Bowdler, Church Stretton, in 1956 and seeing the three-year-old colt Bowdler Begger in one of the sheds that they had up on the hill. I've never seen a prettier pony. He was dark, dappled grey by Bowdler Blue Boy out of Bowdler Bess II. I learnt by example from George that day, how to snare a pony. He had the halter at the end of his long thumb stick and a long line back to his hand. He would slowly stalk the pony until he could reach to drop the halter over his head and then pull the lead tight. My father offered him £450 for Beggar which was a tremendous amount of money in 1956. It was in the era of the legendary Coed Coch Madog. My father was one of the first to put him up as a young horse in the ring but he reckoned that Beggar would have beaten him. George wouldn't sell. Years later at the Tredegar show I was judging Mountain Ponies and this young lady came in with this beautiful blue, dappled, grey stallion but he was so fat. Incredibly fat. However I still couldn't put him any lower than second and I said to the young lady that if she had this pony in better condition he'd not only be winning this class but he'd be winning the championship. 'Well,' she said, 'don't blame me, blame him,' pointing towards my steward, who was Mr Watkins, and the pony was Tafarnaubach Sion, a great grandson of Bowdler Beggar but of course he didn't let on. Years later it was sad to see Beggar as an old pony, looking poor, down on a common in South Wales. I often wonder what might have been had George Preece shaken my father's hand?

On that same visit to Bowdler we saw the mares and bought Bowdler Betty Blue who was a full sister to both Beggar, Brewer and Blighter. She bred us some nice fillies but was eventually sold to Denmark. It was such cold weather so we went back to the house and Mrs Preece had laid out a huge pork pie. I can see it now. She cut it up into four and we ate that with English mustard. I can still taste that pie today. Years later, when George was President of the Welsh Pony and Cob Society in 1976 I had the great pleasure of driving him around the Royal Welsh showground, which was permitted back then, well at least I hope it was! The Bowdler ponies were a unique type and did so much good for so many studs. Emrys Griffiths himself bought Bowdler Brewer and Blighter and they did such tremendous job for him. We had the stallion, Bowdler Banger, by Criban Pilot for a while who was a typical Long Mynd type of pony. He made his way to Belgium. Another from the same bloodlines was the colt foal Rookery Bunting, purchased from Robina Mills in Hay-on-Wye market for 90gns in 1972. He was out of Bowdler Bon-Bon who was by Bowdler Ballistite and had inherited the same dark, rich mahogany bay colour from him. He sired a Fayre Oaks record-priced foal for us in Derwen Eclipse, a black filly, foaled in 1980 and going back to Derwen Enfys, who was by old Clan Dash and out of another Bowdler mare, Bowdler Beautiful II. Eclipse was sold for 900gns which would equate to over £3,500 in today's prices. The worst thing about that day was that we had some beautiful and expensive leather-backed grooming brushes that we took to shows. We thought we'd hidden them whilst we took the ponies through the sale ring, but somebody must have been watching as by the time we had come back to the pen after the sale, somebody had stolen them. There are very few people you can trust.

Another person from that same area around Church Stretton that I looked up to was Dick Swain, Crossways Stud, and I had the honour of singing at his funeral.

Myfanwy was quite successful showing the Mountain Ponies and I think would secretly wished to have kept a few. When we first met she knew little or nothing about horses so the Mountain Ponies were an easier start, being the right size and generally manageable. She quite rightly attributes her knowledge and confidence to my father. When we were first married I would be working in the garage all day, so it was left to my father to teach her, and for Myfanwy to learn from. However one day I arrived home to great consternation. There had been a crowd of visitors to the stud before Lampeter and father had told Myfanwy to bring out Derwen Princess to show her off to them. Now Father always wore a heavy Burberry-type mackintosh. As Myfanwy jogged up the lane with Princess the mackintosh was flapped to liven her up when, of course, Princess took the cue to lift her tail and stride off leaving poor Myfanwy in a heap... with no Cob. Thankfully Princess turned back before she reached the main road and no harm was done, except maybe to Myfanwy's dented pride.

Back in the sixties my father and I bought the stallion Revel Jonas 3440. I can usually remember the registration numbers of the famous ones, from Eric Jones of the Monnow Stud. We paid £3,000 for him. It was a fortune, not only then, in the sixties, but today also. We didn't show him but we had some good stock by him, which you should expect really as he was out of one of the loveliest mares I'd seen in my life, Revel Joain and by Bowdler Blighter. Buying didn't always go to plan, though, as we purchased a lovely pony for a client called Brierwood Lady Killer by Coed Coch Madog from Dai Meredith of the Vaynor Stud. The deal was done over a bottle of brandy Dai had won in a Christmas raffle. On getting home I phoned the intended owner and he said, 'Oh I'm sorry, I've already bought a stallion.' 'Never mind,' I said.

'I never buy anything that I'm not happy to keep myself.' Lady Killer left us some great stock including the Royal Welsh winner, Derwen Boy Blue.

You have to be focused. There's no deviation if you want to be a breeder, but sadly it seems most people are focused on a red rosette as the be-all and end-all today. The great breeders of the past, such as Miss Brodrick, Emrys Griffiths, and Llewellyn Richards, were completely focused on improving the breed and that is why they were successful.

Handsworth Dairies Limited

Head Office and Dairy
ISLAND RD. HANDSWORTH
BIRMINGHAM · 21

Branches:
355 CHESTER ROAD, ERDINGTON
PHONE ERD 0642

SOUTH BIRMINGHAM DAIRIES LTD.
PERSHORE ROAD, SELLY PARK
PHONE SEL. 1102

Directors:
C. WHITE.   F. V. WHITE
A. J. WHITE

Telephone:
NORTHERN 2171 - 2172

PYW/MS.   4th. October 1947

E.H.Lloyd.Esq.,
Garth Villa.
Drefach.
Llanybyther. Cards.

Dear Sir,

    "e have pleasure in enclosing herewith
our cheque for £145. being the price agreed
yesterday for the mare we purchased from you.

    "e shall be glad to have your receipt
on the back of the cheque, which is all the
acknowledgement required.

       Yours faithfully,
       for. HANDSWORTH DAIRIES. LD.

        W.C.White

Chapter Three

Buying and Selling
'Remember this – breeding horses will never make you rich. Keeping cobs is a labour of love.'

From my childhood days I would accompany my father on his buying expeditions. I vividly remember going with him to Merthyr and standing outside the Hoover factory. The common land in front of the factory was a parking place back then. There I spotted a white pony and its foal grazing. My father fancied the pony at once and I asked him how he would be able to find the owner. There was no one around.

In the town my father stopped outside a milk bottling plant. Someone there would surely know something about the pony and foal. I went over and I asked the very first person I saw. I was rather shy but, as it turned out, he was the owner! Off we went, my father and I and the owner to haggle in a pub in nearby Dowlais. As they debated for over three hours I sat sipping lemonade and eating crisps in the car. My father succeeded in buying the pony and later sold it on to someone in America, the first of many exports.

I would accompany my father everywhere during the sixties on his journeys and visits while he inspected ponies, assessing their entitlement and grading them for inclusion in the Foundation Stock register of the Welsh Stud Book. One of the first breeders we visited was Gerwyn James, Rhosmaen, Crymych, who bred the Carnalw ponies under the gaze of the Preseli Hills. As a result of that visit we became very friendly with the James family, over the years buying many of his ponies for export. Gerwyn often used our stallions when he bred the occasional Cob. One son of Derwen Quartz, Carnalw Bobby was bought by two sisters in Essex who had tremendous success with him. Father and he got on very well, both being shrewd farmers with a lot of respect for each other.

Such visits helped me make friends with characters all over Wales. My father would often travel to the Brynaman area. Every time we crossed the Black Mountain I would sing a song popularised by Bois y Blacbord, a choir conducted by Noel John. '*Dros y Mynydd Du i Frynaman*' ('Over the Black Mountain to Brynaman').

There I would meet characters like Dylan Jones, Tomi Joci, Coth, Ifan Oliver, Eta Moses and Thomas Cwm Triwpit. I would know most of them by their nicknames. These were miners, milkmen and farmers but, above all, genuine horsemen who had been breeding Mountain Ponies from childhood. Singing was to open up a whole new world for me which I imagine, unconsciously at the time, broke down any barriers to the worldwide influence of the Derwen Cob Stud.

Singing became an increasingly important part of my life. My years of following the eisteddfod circuit were hectic years. At weekends especially I would seldom be home. 1968 was a particularly successful year for me, winning a scholarship awarded at Pontrhydfendigaid by Glynne Jones. This resulted in my being invited to tour North America with the choir accompanying Beverly Humphreys from Pontypridd. This meant travelling 18,000 miles in sixteen days on planes, buses and ships. Three years later I was invited again, this time to Canada. I remember crossing the Rockies from Vancouver to Edmonton by train. Naturally, the train was a 'sleeper'. It stopped overnight among the Rockies where we slept. I got up early and went to the restaurant car for an orange juice and came across an unexpected sight. In the car at the counter there was a queue of Native Americans bartering fresh salmon and pheasants for whiskey and cigarettes. I decided to visit their reservation. They presented me with a heavy and thick knitted coat with the tribe's totem being an integral part of the design. That coat is among my greatest treasures.

I will never forget that journey way back in 1968. My first experience of the New World was landing in bright sunshine on Baffin Island. This was followed by a four-hour flight to Vancouver International Airport. We spent a few days in British Columbia were we sang to an audience of 4,000 people. We also appeared on national television. In Vancouver we performed to another huge audience of 3,000 people.

It is strange how a seemingly mundane incident at the time seems to linger in the memory. In New York State I met an exiled Welshman who was in his seventies, Robat Griffiths. He had left Wales for America with his parents when he was only three years old. His only opportunity to converse in Welsh was at the annual St David's Day celebrations with other exiles. Yet his Welsh remained as fluent as ever. But another exile, a lady who had only left Aberystwyth eight years previously, had lost her Welsh completely. I still remember the two different attitudes reflected by those two people. There is a lesson there somewhere.

There is an old Welsh proverb that claims that the best Welshman is an exiled Welshman. I would not go as far as to agree with that, although it may hold some truth. But I could adapt that proverb to state that the saddest Welshman is a Welshman abroad. As we performed Welsh songs, and as we chatted to these Welsh exiles, the tears would inevitably flow. The year before I visited Canada and America for the first time, Tom Jones' 'Green, Green Grass of Home' had reached the charts. It was a song that tugged at the heartstrings of any exiled Welsh people, despite the fact that it was an American song. But Tom was a Welshman and, to these exiles, many of them descendants of the early pioneers, the green, green grass of home was in Wales.

Between the two singing tours I was honoured by being inaugurated as a member of the Gorsedd, thus emulating my grandfather Daniel Jenkins. The Gorsedd of the Bards is an association made up of poets, writers, musicians, artists and other people who have made a distinguished contribution to the Welsh nation, the language, and its culture. Members in their druidic robes meet every year on the National Eisteddfod field. Members adopt a bardic name and at the Flint Eisteddfod in 1970 I was honoured and chose the name 'Aeronfab' meaning Son of the Aeron.

Another eisteddfod honour I was fortunate to achieve was at the Llangollen International Eisteddfod, winning the Singer of the Year award, a feat synonymous with winning the National Eisteddfod's Blue Ribbon award for soloists.

Soon afterwards I was invited to sing at the Royal Albert Hall at a St David's Day concert. The concert was organised to celebrate the fiftieth anniversary of Urdd Gobaith Cymru (The

Welsh League of Youth). It was not a new experience for me. I had performed at the Albert Hall the previous year with Dafydd Edwards as part of a London Welsh St David's Day concert.

Following some success on stage, and on the radio and television, I was approached by Dennis Rees of Wren Records, the leading Welsh recording company of the time. He offered me a contract to record an album. I accepted and it was released in October 1968. On the last day of that month it reached number eight in the bestsellers chart in *Y Cymro*. The following week it was at number seven!

The recording was made at the BBC studio in Alexandra Road, Swansea with my old singing teacher Ted Morgan as my accompanist. It was a straightforward process in those days. We did not have to be segregated in different rooms. I just stood in front of the microphone beside the piano while Ted played, exactly as if I was on stage. The engineer was in the next room behind a huge window. We recorded four tracks in two hours.

The weekly top ten list in *Y Cymro* was the definitive Welsh language records chart in those days. It appeared weekly and elicited much rivalry between pop singers and groups. It is interesting to note that the record at number two when my album entered the charts was a Welsh version of 'Something Simple' sung by Mary Hopkin. Her song 'Those Were the Days' reached number one in the English charts that same year.

I was paid £18. 3s. 6d. for my work but the money was nothing compared to the prestige of being a recorded artiste. The record sold 1,050 copies in twelve months for which I received a royalty payment of £8.

I did in fact enter a recording studio many years later in 2004 to record a CD that reflected my singing career over the years. I recorded it at Fflach Studios in Cardigan accompanied by Eirian Owen. Once again I chose some of the old favourites, and why not? They had served me well. Among popular Welsh hymns I included English songs such as 'God Keep You in My Prayer', 'Were You There?' 'If I Can Help Somebody', 'I'll Walk Beside You' and 'Mary's Boy Child'. That to me was my last act musically. That metaphorically was my final curtain.

The CD cover photograph pictures me with Derwen Replica on the beach at Newquay, thus uniting two of the main components that have made me what I am today.

The relationship between man and his steed is inexplicable. It becomes something that is inborn. There is a story regarding my father at Llanybydder mart with Dilwyn Edwards, one of the three Edwards brothers from Pontrhydygroes who transported farm animals. Dilwyn was holding the reins of a rather tall horse when my father advised him to step back. He did and immediately the horse collapsed like a felled tree. It was dead before it hit the ground. If it hadn't been for my father's warning, the horse would have fallen on Dilwyn. How did my father know that such a thing was about to happen? His explanation was, 'I didn't like the look in his eye.'

Dilwyn still remembers that incident and recognises his debt to my father.

There is a special way to treat a horse. One important aspect is never to raise your voice. Whenever anyone loads a horse onto a lorry or trailer, they should never berate the animal. Everything should be done benignly. By losing patience with a horse you agitate yourself in the process. This in turn agitates the horse and he will react accordingly.

When my father would call at Pentrefelin to meet Mam, when

they were courting, he would be wary of the bees kept by Daniel Jenkins, his future father-in-law. My father would invariably be stung while my grandfather would always be unscathed. Grandfather's advice to my father would be, 'Don't get worked up!' The same is true when handling horses. The handler's voice, smell and feel are all important factors. And when a horse is shown in the ring it must be made to realise that its handler is also its best friend. Patience is the keyword when handling a horse. Without patience you stand no chance.

When I finished in the garage in 1985 I said to Myfanwy, 'What are we going to do now?' and she quickly replied that the only other thing I knew anything about was horses. So we started from scratch, buying and selling, and soon we were exporting a lorry load of Welsh Ponies or Cobs every six weeks. One of the early lessons we learnt from a seller's and buyer's point of view was that it was essential that every animal we dealt with was able to load in and out of a trailer or a lorry. We spent a lot of time training the ones that wouldn't, but it was time well spent. From 1985 up to 2008 I mostly sold Ponies, Cobs and horses privately relying on the Derwen Stud's reputation. The selling circle widened as our reputation spread far and wide. In 2008 I reached that age when I could travel freely on buses, and Myfanwy and I decided it was time we took life a little easier. We reduced the number of our cobs. I realised that this would be a wise move, that and reviewing our *modus operandi.*

On return trips from the continent I would often call in with Rose and Joe Hardwick of the Tuscany Stud, just alongside the Severn Bridge in Avonmouth. During one of these stops in 1986 Rose suggested that we go out to exhibit at the International Show in Aachen, Germany, later that year. I said to her that she must be crazy but as the evening went on we decided to go halves on the cost. She would take her ridden Cob, Gerrig Gem, and we would take Derwen Tawela, who had a colt foal at foot – Derwen Tennessee Express. All went well and the colt was champion foal. A young blonde Swedish lady came up to us and looked interested. With the help of Inger Becker translating, whose English was perfect, they asked if he was in fact for sale. I said yes, which pleased them but, she announced that first she had to clear it with her father. Off they went and several other people showed an interest in him too, including a man from Luxembourg who was most put out that he couldn't just have him, asking what was wrong with his money? I explained that I had given my word to the initial young lady, but when I didn't hear back from her that night I thought I'd fluffed the sale. However all was good as she did come back in the morning and said her father had agreed she could buy him. What transpired was that she had phoned home, 'Father, Father, I am in love!' 'What about your partner Sture? He replied. 'No, no, it's a foal!' The rest is history as that was 34-year-old Gunn Johansson of the Burhults Stud who has become such a great friend, and through her we have sold many animals to Sweden over the last 30 years.

One order we had in 1993 was for 42 Mountain Ponies to go to Malta through a Mr Cassar. He was known as 'The Animal Man' as at that time he was the one who controlled the import/export licences for animals on and off the island. The means by which we gained a foothold in Malta is worth repeating. It happened through soloist Eirios Thomas, Tregaron, who was living on the island at the time. Coincidentally a relative of Myfanwy's, Sarah Melita Davies had lived on Malta for many years. Having toured the main opera houses of Europe she was made 'chief prima

donna' at the Royal Opera House in Malta, returning to London
in 1923 to sing for the Prince of Wales, in Welsh, English and
Italian, accompanied by the band of the Royal Welsh Guards.

Obviously with such an undertaking I was in regular contact
with the Ministry of Agriculture here, and a very nice lady called
Mrs Smith, whom I never actually met. However, one day she
phoned and she said, 'Mr Lloyd, we've been having a lot of interest
in this consignment as people have been saying that they are to
be travelled in transport trucks?' I had to tell her that I genuinely
didn't know as everything was being organised by 'The Animal
Man'. Well the day came for departure, and the trucks arrived,
like a road train, so long that we had to take the trailer part off
and bring it up on the tractor. Each unit had feed bins and water
troughs along the one side so we had no reason to worry.

This was a case of history repeating itself in one way as in
1958/59 father had sold 36 Mountain Ponies to a Hugh Steward
in Ontario, Canada.

In 1985 we sold a horse to France, Derwen Duke of York. I
intended keeping him but I needed money for replacing a new
roof on the house. Over the years it had decayed and the repair
was a necessity. Both Myfanwy and I are indebted to Duke of York
for the roof over our heads. I can still see the French dormobile
arriving on the yard. Out stepped Robert and Christine Granger.
He didn't speak a word of English other than 'Welsh Cob' but
Christine did. Off we went around the foals and Duke of York
was fast asleep. Suddenly on seeing us, he sat up, and stretched
and rose to his feet. Robert said straight away. 'Oui, oui!' and I
replied, 'Non, non!'

We had a great time with the French visitors and Myfanwy
had cooked a lovely roast lunch which they really enjoyed as they

said it was the first home-cooked lunch they'd had since they'd been in Great Britain as everywhere seemed to be serving lettuce and salad!

The talk kept coming back to that of the foal, so I said to Myfanwy, 'If the cost of the roof was £6,000 then that's what they'll have to pay, which of course they won't.' Of course they said 'Oui!' He was sold on one condition – that if they ever wished to sell him I was to be offered first refusal, which of course they did and he returned to Ynyshir in 1995.

Robert was a monoglot Frenchman. My French was confined to the few words I had been taught at school. The day I travelled out to collect Duke, Christine, who was a doctor, invited me to visit a vineyard. I gladly accepted. Off we went, Robert driving his old Citroen 2CV, a car more suitable for a hippy than a millionaire. He was squeezed into this tiny car as he was a huge man. With the aid of a French-English dictionary I managed to communicate with him. I had no idea where we were heading and so we arrived at a place I had never heard of called Epernay. There at Number 20, Avenue de Champagne, I saw a sign that said 'Moet et Chandon'. We entered and joined a party of some two dozen people for a tour of the premises. We, however, were taken by a representative on a personal tour. He and Robert were close friends, both sharing a love of driving horses.

It was an amazing place. It produced 26 million bottles of champagne a year. We were shown the whole process from beginning to end. Filling the bottles was not the end of the process. Every day the stored bottles had to be turned. We were then led up to Napoleon's Room. It was there, apparently, that the Emperor regularly relaxed over a glass of bubbly. Outside the window grew a yew tree that had been there since Napoleon's days. On the table in front of us stood a magnum of Dom Perignon. Unfortunately, following a fullsome breakfast I had to make do with just one glass. Had I known better I would have readily forsaken breakfast that day!

Around the same time in 1984 we took a number of breeders and their Cobs out to the International Welsh Pony and Cob Show in Ermelo in the Netherlands. The display, which included 23 stallions in all, was well organised by Dan Haak. I took Derwen Replica, and a visiting German enthusiast asked to take his photograph. Later a German breeder, Jurgen Wiemers, came over to Pennant and began dealing with us. Having got acquainted with him I discovered he had been a miner who had diversified into producing concrete moulds used in motorway construction. This venture made him a millionaire and over the years Jurgen bought some twelve stallions, primarily for driving, from us. They included Derwen Sherlock Holmes, a Replica son who became European and seven-times German singles driving champion with his nephew Steffan Wiemers. He did extremely well with the stallions he bought from us, eventually breeding his own to train for harness work on a beautiful property in Germany. He sent us a letter that we kept:

Letter from Families Wiemers, Germany.

Dear Ivor,

I would like to use the occasion of your International Meeting on Derwen Stut in 1990 to dedicate this photo album to you.

Exactly five years ago I purchased the first two of the total of twelve horses with you. After five years I can now give a short report about my experience with Welsh Horses.

Being one of only few people in Germany watching his Welsh Cob, Sek C and D in comparison to the performance of other races in tournaments, I take the liberty to judge as follows;

In the long run you only have a chance with highest quality; I am very glad to know you as a breeder and salesman who is well aware of quality. It is a fact that your horses were expensive, but they are worth it. "Family Weimers" has become a quality mark for carriage sports. More than 100 triumphs are evident.

We are not only demanded in shows but we are celebrated; wherever there are cups to be won for good hitching up, it is our turn...

.... Dear Ivor, we wish you, your family and your stud as well as your business affairs a good future."

Sadly, although he didn't smoke or drink he died suddenly at only 65 years of age.

Derwen Rebound was purchased unseen by American breeder Gordon Heard of the Crossroads Stud, then in New Hampshire and eventually Virginia. Rebound was a son of Derwen Rosina's Last and Derwen Rosie and was secured as his pedigree could be traced directly back to the late 1920s and the illustrious Ceitho Welsh Comet. This had been traced back to Mr Heard's satisfaction by Joan Curry of the Pontllys Stud who at the time offered a pedigree research service. She accompanied Rebound on his flight to America.

Derwen Serenllys by Rosina's Last was another international ambassador for the stud and its bloodlines when he set off to Mary Willsallen in New South Wales, Australia in 1974. Both colts being pioneers in setting up Welsh Cob interest in these countries.

One day I received a phone call completely out of the blue from another American. His name was Owen C. Glenn and he was with his wife Suzanne at Fishguard and about to leave Wales following a holiday. His message was that he just couldn't leave Wales without seeing the Derwen Cobs. They had happened to visit an antique shop kept by a friend of ours, Barry Thomas, a well-known television cameraman I had often worked with. Barry had told them all about our horses. It was towards the end of autumn and after they returned to America, Owen called again. He had decided to buy Suzanne two Cobs as a present. We struck a bargain and the Cobs were flown out to California in time for Christmas Eve. They were Derwen Dashing Duke (Derwen Replica x Derwen Duchess) and Derwen Tequila (Derwen Replica x Derwen Telynores). These were the first of many that they bought from us, including the highly successful driven Cob Derwen True Grit (Derwen Requiem x Derwen True Story).

Another married couple who opened doors for us abroad were Penti and Kirsty Lehtonen from Finland who had seen photographs of our Cobs in a German riding magazine in 1990. We arranged that I would travel with the eight Cobs that they had purchased to the port at Harwich where I would meet Penti. He would bring his own lorry and we would load the horses and take them to the quarantine quarters for clearance before he would board the ship with his lorry and load. It was a merchant ship carrying timber but, again, both the ship and the lorry had been adapted for transporting horses as well.

However proficient someone is in breeding and selling and buying horses, fate still remains an important factor. The old adage of being in the right place at the right time is no figment of the imagination. Like most clichés, it has a strong element of truth. I was at a sale at Llanelwedd some 30 years ago. A horse was led into the ring that was from our stud's bloodline. Opposite us were a crew of young women who seemed intent on buying it and they succeeded.

The following year we visited Rhandirmwyn show and there, under saddle, was the very same horse we had seen at the sale. The buyer was still a stranger to me but she turned to our head stable girl at the time, Karin Fjeldbo from Denmark, asking her for some practical advice before entering the ring. Karin readily obliged and the horse won first prize. The owner was so pleased that she invited us to join her at the Royal Oak pub to celebrate.

It was only then that we discovered her identity. She was Ari Ashley, the world famous designer Laura Ashley's daughter-in-law. She and her husband Nick, Laura's son, became very good friends of ours. A year later we organised an open day on our farm and hundreds turned up. About an hour before the event began we received a telephone call. It was Ari enquiring about our open day. She wanted to know whether there was a suitable place where they could land their helicopter.

The family owned a summer cottage near Llanelwedd and within half an hour they were with us. Even in those days, a helicopter was not a very common occurrence and to those who attended the open day, seeing one landing at close quarters was a rare sight.

A few years later, Ari called again. She asked us whether we would sell a horse on her behalf. It was that very same horse that had brought us together. She was expecting a child and she had been ordered by Nick not to undertake any riding until the child had been born. We agreed to help her and did so willingly without charge. As a token of appreciation she invited us out to dinner at her father-in-law's place. She referred to it as 'Daddy's hotel'. Daddy, of course, was daddy-in-law Sir Bernard Ashley and we soon found ourselves at Llangoed Hall near Erwood in Powys.

As we arrived we were met with an amazing sight. The car park was full of Ferraris and Lamborghinis. As it happened a son of one of our friends was employed there as a concierge. John Thomas' duties included ushering guests into the stately home and ensuring them a warm welcome. For this he would be generously tipped with many a £50 note pressed into his palm. According to John, the best tippers were the Chinese. Among the gentry present there were common folk like us. Another was a local character known as 'Dai the Milk', who just happened to be a close friend of Sir Bernard.

Over the years we have sold a number of Cobs to Denmark as well and so Dewi Rosina's descendants inhabit countries throughout Europe. By now we have exported our cobs to eighteen countries, including one Cob to Japan. I remember putting animals on the train in Llandovery to Tilbury Docks and then off to the Continent. When Derwen Serenllys went to Australia on a ship it took him six weeks. Derwen is by now a truly internationally famous prefix.

The highlight of my life was meeting Myfanwy on that day in Llandovery, though another highlight was and still is meeting people from all walks of life. Everyone knows that eleven o'clock is coffee time at Derwen so we're always in the house, so it's a good time to meet, in fact at one time our house always seemed to be full of people. In the days of the Llanarth sale, and when there wasn't an auction on the Sunday at Builth, it was nothing to have 40-50 visitors for tea.

The thirteenth Llanarth sale in 1976 was a lucky one for us and for Russell Baldwin & Bright auctioneers who recorded it as their most successful event at the venue to date. We took the yearling colt, Derwen Arwr by Derwen Rosina's Last out of Brynymor Aurwen, the full sister to Brynymor Welsh Magic. He sold for 1600gns, (approximately £13,500 in today's money) to a Canadian buyer, Peter Carter, but remained near Ruthin with his brother-in-law Bernard Woolford, Coed-y-Parc.

The following year we went one better by capturing the two highest price sales. The chestnut yearling colt Derwen Trysor (Derwen Llwynog x Derwen Seren Teledu) made 1500gns to Laurie Harrison's, Oughtrington Stud, near Lymm in Cheshire, with 1400gns being paid for the bay filly foal, Derwen Last's Request (Derwen Rosina's Last x Tydi Rosita) by Dennis Bushby of the Buckswood Stud. The average price that day was 316gns.

There was a definite decline in visitors when the Llanarth sale ended and the Cob sale moved to Builth Wells so we'd hoped to build up our own sale at home but sadly the overall standard on offer from the guest consignors after our first reduction in 1981 was not of sufficient quality to draw the buyers so we decided not to carry on. That first sale which had only our own animals on offer saw 54 entries, mainly Cobs but also some Mountain Ponies. Top of the sale was the beautiful Derwen King Last (Derwen Rosina's Last x Derwen Queen) who was a big winner as a yearling in 1978, but he was sold as a gelding to performance enthusiast Megan Lewis for 1,900gns who is now better known for her Cwrt-y-Cadno Section B's. The five-year-old Derwen Princess daughter, Derwen Perl, topped the mares at 1,500gns to

Idris James, Hendrewen who re-offered her for sale as a thirteen-year-old where she was bought by Peter Grey, Thorneyside, for 4,400gns who then re-sold her as an 18-year-old for 4,000gns to go to American breeder Suzanne Glenn. However Lot 34 failed to make her reserve by just 50gns so we decided to retain her as a gift for our soon-to-be-born son Dyfed. This was Derwen Groten Goch, the mare who later went on to be three-time Prince of Wales Cup winner! Sometimes it pays dividends to stick to your selling price.

The interest in good quality animals has increased and the interest in less good animals has decreased, and that's why we strive to breed as good quality as we can at all times. In 2017 we sold a gelding to a lady from Henley-on-Thames called Wendy James who had purchased from us before. She's having him trained with Karen Crago, who was a pupil of Carl Hester, so we're looking forward very much to him coming out under saddle. But within two hours of selling him we had an email from Australia for him. Just from his photo appearing on the website, not even offering him for sale, purely as it was a good photo. I suppose the internet is having an effect but we tend to sell by 'word of mouth' and through people who have bought before, satisfied customers who have then recommended us to other purchasers.

One thing I've always stuck to and that is 'pure breeding'. By now the numbers are sufficient to stop allowing crossing the sections. We should only breed within the section, so C x C = C and D x D = D. I'm a great believer in that. Personally I'm quite happy with the Welsh Part-Bred section being only of 12.5% Welsh blood, as the part-bred is what it is. If someone wants to produce a bigger, faster animal then the part-bred is the obvious alternative, but by diluting it too much you don't necessarily retain that good temperament of the pure bred.

We did deal in various general riding animals of various types and breeds from time to time, having been tipped off by the various 'bird dogs' we had around the country, like football scouts keeping an eye open for good animals that we might be interested in. We had four or five of these contacts who I would give a bottle or two of something to for finding anything we might like. One such 'bird dog' was Tom Roberts down in South Wales who found us a grand mare called Rose. When we went to see her she was standing on the street. I shall always remember when he took her back to her stable she had to walk down a flight of steps to go underneath the house she was living in, which was alongside the river where she would be led to get washed down. It was unbelievable, you could do anything with her. Another big horse was a handsome dun Highland cross called Berti who came via Llanybydder mart. A grand sort, hard to find these days.

Remember this – breeding horses will never make you rich. Keeping Cobs is a labour of love. It is also a pure joy that has brought me immense pleasure. It has been a privilege to share that joy and pleasure with close family, kind neighbours and good friends throughout the world.

Like most people who have horses, they have dogs and cats too. We were no different. As well as writing about our Cobs, I should also mention some of the dogs that have shared my life over the years. I have previously mentioned my first dog, the Jack Russell that my mother named Two Bob because that's how much he cost me to buy. The first family dog arrived much later. It was a Spaniel called Lassie. Our son Dyfed was born during the heavy snowfalls of 1981. We were left with no electricity and the only fire was the

Myfanwy and myself
on the mountain
near Tregaron.

Noson Lawen in the indoor riding school.

Part of the museum that
Myfanwy created.

Students attending one of the
"Introduction to the Welsh Cob"
lectures.

Brierwood Lady Killer by Coed Coch Madog, sire of Royal
Welsh winner Derwen Boy Blue out of Bowdler Buss.

Myfanwy at Pontrhyfendigaid Show, 1976 with Derwen Dot
by Clan Gylen out of Derwen Delight.

Derwen Delight, out of Criban Leading Lady, dam of the stallion Derwen Planed's Delight.

Rookery Bunting purchased as a foal from Hay-on-Wye sale.

Derwen Eclipse, by Rookery Bunting, top price filly foal at the Fayre Oaks sale.

Derwen Groten Goch as a
brood mare at home, in the
show ring, and as a yearling.
Opposite – Dyfed and myself
with the Prince of Wales
Cup and her Championship
rosettes from 1986 and 1992.

Derwen Quartz winning at Pembrokeshire County Show ridden by Marina Lundin and then out with his mares overlooking Cardigan Bay.

Derwen Mr T in Sweden at the Burhults Stud, by Quartz out of Derwen Tawela by Derwen Llwynog.

Derwen Two Rivers, Champion at Cardigan Show with Gemma Gooding who also partnered Derwen Requiem, below.

Derwen Duke of York, by Derwen Replica ridden by Marina Lundin.

Derwen Sea Adventurer by Tireinon Step-On, successful in harness.

Derwen Cantona by Aston Dynamite being driven in Spain.

The stallions Derwen Denmark and Derwen True Grit competing in California for Suzanne Moody.

Derwen Red Marvel by Nebo Black Magic, a successful sire of part-breds in Leicestershire for George Coombes and Hilary Legard who rode him in the 1984 Olympia display.

The stallions, Derwen Two Rivers and Texas Express making themselves useful on the farm by herding up the cattle.

Tireinon Confidence by Derwen Railway Express on the day we purchased him, seen here with Neil and David Wray and his breeder Roy Higgins.

Tireinon Step On as a colt with Wynford Higgins at the Royal Welsh Show.

A two year old Derwen Telynor with Nelson Smith at the Trevallion Stud near Coventry, where he became a much valued sire.

Derwen Desert Express by Derwen Railway Express at Lampeter Stallion Show 1989 with his owner David Llewellyn.

With our good friend Gunn Johansson of the Burhults Stud.

Derwen Gladstone by Derwen Prince Charming, in 2017 on his return from Gunn Johansson in Sweden with his personal groom Elin.

Our senior stallion Derwen Revelation in front of the old "Gambo". Foaled in 1996, he has a double cross of Derwen Replica.

Derwen Reason by Derwen Revelation winning at Lampeter Stallion Show with Daniel Hughes (Ionos Stud). Reason has four crosses of Derwen Replica.

Derwen Revelation.

Derwen Replica at Glanusk Stallion Show.

The cheque I received from the W.P.C.S. as compensation for the unfounded accusation against me.

Derwen Dusk photographed in 2017 with Toni Rooney from Australia.

Our prizewinning foal of 2017, Derwen Twilight by Derwen Dusk with W.P.C.S. Young Ambassador, Euros Llŷr Morgan.

My cousin Richard Molineux with his stained glass designed harp trophy presented to the W.P.C.S. Young Ambassador.

Derwen Railway Express, when in the ownership of the Batt family, Abergavenny Stud. Pictured here aged 24 at the Glanusk Park Parade and Art exhibition, 2002.

Derwen True Grit by Derwen Requiem at the Glenhaven Stud in the USA.

one in the parlour. We had only just brought Dyfed home from hospital and Myfanwy had placed him in his pram in the warmth of the parlour. Half an hour later, Lassie came in and cocked her ears outside the parlour door. She knew there was an addition to the family inside and in she went. From that moment, Dyfed and Lassie were inseparable. Unfortunately she was rather boisterous and tended to jump around while playing with Dyfed. After she pushed him down the front door steps we unfortunately had to give her away to friends of ours who gave her a good home.

The next family dog was another bitch, a Doberman called Kitty. Dyfed by then was five years old. The reason we bought Kitty was the fact that we lived in a rather remote area and needed a guard dog. As one who was used to studying Cob pedigrees I decided to do the same with the Doberman breed. I read that the best pedigree at the time was the Tavy line. We had friends, Stephanie Edwards and Paul Taylor, who lived close to very good breeding kennels so they kindly went on our behalf to view the dogs. They looked in particular for a good natured dog. As soon as the breeder opened the kennel doors, out came a bitch. She jumped up and placed her front paws on Stephanie's shoulders and licked her face. She was so tall that she stood eye-to-eye with Steph, who realised immediately that one of her pups would be perfect; and so Kitty came to live at Ynyshir. 'Hey, Kitty! Kitty! Kitty!' would be heard constantly from either Dyfed, Myfanwy or myself. Any stranger approaching the yard would think we were calling a cat and would be shocked to see a large black bitch running around.

Our next canine was yet again a bitch, this time a Rhodesian Ridgeback with a black stripe running down her back. This was Tess, and I have to admit that she was rather dim. Later on a sheepdog arrived, Rex from Nantgaredig. I went there to buy a horse and as I approached the farm I had to pull in to allow a tractor to pass. Sitting in the cab with the driver was a dog. I stopped to chat to the driver and complimented him on the condition of his dog. He said, with pride, that this dog, Bob, was the most intelligent dog in the neighbourhood. He demonstrated what he meant. He ordered the dog to walk up the road and stop. The dog obeyed. He commanded him to jump into the trailer. Bob obeyed. I was impressed and said I would be interested in buying one of his offspring. In fact the farmer, Peter Brown, had a litter of Bob's pups. I returned to Nantgaredig a few days later and the litter was there, playing in the trailer. One of them jumped out and ran towards me, a black and tan not unlike the traditional Welsh sheepdog. Mrs Brown had already named him Rex.

I placed Rex in a cardboard box in the boot of my car and headed back for home. On the way I stopped to do some shopping at Aberaeron and as I returned to the car I could hear Rex barking loudly. He made himself known immediately.

Rex was with us for 15 years. He wasn't a working dog but he became very defensive of Myfanwy. He was a very obedient dog. He never rushed towards his bowl when he was being fed. He always waited until told to eat. He was gentle and faithful and never left the yard. Dyfed idolised him and would often say, 'Rex is the only dog and I'm the only child. But no one understands us!'

We kept cats as pets as well. Among them were tail-less Manx Cats. The first of these was Soot, on account of her colour of course. Then came Soot II and then a ginger cat named Ginge. And then then came the family favourite, Cwta, Welsh for 'short', an appropriate name for a cat with just a stump for a tail. Cwta became a television star, appearing on a magazine programme televised from the Tinopolis Studio in Llanelli. I rang the researcher informing her of a possible story for the programme. At nearby Llangennech, Eirwyn and Laura Hughes bred Manx cats. In fact it was from them that I bought Cwta. The couple with some of their cats, including Cwta, were invited to the studio. I was afraid that Cwta would try to escape from the bright lights of the studio but no, she was as good as gold and behaved impeccably. She was a natural television celebrity. Top Cat!

THE ROYAL WELSH AGRICULTURAL SOCIETY Ltd

Cymdeithas Amaethyddol Frenhinol Cymru Cyf.

Patron :
Her Majesty The Queen

Chairman of Council :
Col. J. F. Williams-Wynne,
C.B.E., D.S.O., M.A., F.R.Ag.S.

Secretary-Manager :
J. Arthur George,
F.R.Ag.S., D.B.H.S., A.C.I.S.

LLANELWEDD, Builth Wells,
Breconshire LD2 3SY
Telephone : Builth Wells 3683/4/5

Your Ref.

Our Ref.
Date as Postmark.

Dear Mr Lloyd,

ROYAL WELSH SHOW – 1974 JULY 23RD. 24TH & 25TH

It gives me great pleasure to invite you to Judge the

............WELSH COBS.(Section 'D'.)...............................

of the above exhibition.

A fee of £3. 15 per day is offered for judging, together with the
equivalent of a first class railway fare from your nearest railway
station to Llandrindod Wells station.

This invitation is extended to you provided you have not already
accepted to Judge this breed at The Royal Show of England, The Bath
and West Agricultural Show, The Three Counties Agricultural Show
or The Shropshire and West Midland Show or at any other show in Wales
held prior to the "Royal Welsh".

We look forward to your reply in the near future.

Yours sincerely,

Secretary/Manager

P.S.
On receipt of your reply reservation for accommodation will be communicated
to you after the date and time of the competition is confirmed by the Committee.

Chapter Four

Showing and Judging
'There is a gift to showing successfully.'

I was quite good as an athlete. In fact I was the second-fastest sprinter in Llandeilo School. My son Dyfed inherited this particular talent of being able to run speedily. Sports were part of Rhandirmwyn show and Dyfed used to compete there.

I was around 18 years old when I was first allowed into the main ring at the Royal Welsh. My father frequented all the local marts and at Tregaron in 1960 he chanced upon Davies, Coed Llys, Llanilar, in the Talbot Inn. As they chatted, Davies casually asked him why he had never bought anything from him. He went as far as saying, 'If I buy you a drink will you come and visit?' Never one to turn down such an offer a plan was hatched.

My father visited Coed Llys later with some of the lads from Pant, Llanddewi Brefi. At Coed Llys, David and Marian brought some horses over from the moor and on first glance nothing much appealed, until he spotted a bay colt foal, covered in a thick hairy coat who hadn't been weaned off his mother. A deal was struck and the foal changed hands for £35. Davies made arrangements to hand over the foal at Tregaron mart the following week.

At that time there were no horses sold at Tregaron mart and when the local farmers saw this hairy specimen they lightly mocked my father. They believed that he had, for once, slipped up. The foal was taken to his new home at Derwen Fawr and every weekend my father and I would take it down to a pool in the Cothi River. He loved frolicking in the water, he would roll and wallow and really enjoyed it. With the arrival of spring he lost the hairy coat. It grew a new coat tinged with some brindle reverting to his distant roan relatives, Blaenwaun Trotting Briton, the little roan mare Blaenwaun Flora Temple and her grey sire, Blaenwaun High Stepping Gambler.

The following year the 1961 Royal Welsh was held at Gelli Aur, between Carmarthen and Llandeilo, where I was a student at the time. That year we didn't check into the 'Straw Hotel' as we used to call sleeping over at the Royal Welsh. That's when I was allowed into the main ring for the very first time. I still have photographs to remind me of that great day taken by my mother on her beloved Brownie camera that she took with her everywhere.

In those days there were no separate classes for yearling colts and fillies. We were all in together – I was in the main ring leading this colt! The judge was the legendary Dafydd Edwardes of Tanffynnon, Penuwch. I was told later that there was one competitor in my class who was convinced that he would take home the winner's rosette.

Sharing the main ring back then in another area would be larger and heavier mounted horses. When I entered the ring these became rather agitated. This in turn excited the colt, never having been off the farm before. He arched his tail high over his back and pranced around – showing off. The timing was perfect and Edwardes had no choice but to call him in to take first place position. Edwardes, however, was not entirely satisfied. He asked me to take the colt round the ring again. His explanation was that he needed to ensure that the colt's behaviour hadn't been a fluke. Off I went and, as luck would have it, the mounted horses again became agitated, exciting the colt. Once again, up went the colt's tail as he pranced around playing to the gallery. Again he was called in to the top position by Edwardes. He won the class. That was the first of Coedllys Stardust's many successes.

There is a gift to showing successfully. You can be taught the basics but I believe it to be something more than that, rather an inherent gift. There are also tricks, and no one was better at that than Jack Meiarth, Bwlchllan. Jack, I should point out, usually won legitimately and deservingly, but there were some occasions when he would maybe win third prize by pleading ignorance. If he was not pulled in the ribbons he would sneak into third place hoping the judge and the steward would not realise that he was in the wrong position. Should he be challenged he would apologise profusely swearing that he had misheard the judge. Jack was one of the horse world's true characters.

In 1962 the Royal Welsh was held at Wrexham where Stardust, the roan colt, was again successful, this time under the leading authority Llewellyn Richards, who was heard to remark that he was just the type of Cob he'd be happy to go to war on! My father sold him for £400 to Ann Wheatcroft, the well-known English Cob breeder of the Llanarth (E) / Sydenham Stud who had been having tremendous success with another roan at that time, Llanarth Brummel, also stemming from Blaenwaun Flora Temple.

Stardust's bloodline still remains in our cobs as Stardust's sire was Pentre Eiddwen Comet, the Dewi Rosina's grandson, and before he left for England he sired Derwen Seren in 1963 who went on to produce Replica and Requiem. Thus the picture was completed. Everything my father bought harked back to that first black Cob, Dewi Rosina which he bought in 1944 and his decisions live with us to this day.

I have been blessed with a good memory, and that to me is an important gift. When my father lived at Garth Villa in Drefach in the forties, owning no more than 20 acres of land, he depended on horses for his livelihood. One day he attended a sale at a certain farm. As he arrived the sale was already under way and in the ring was a Collier of around 14 hands. The Collier is a small, squat and hardy type of pony that traditionally worked underground in the coalmines. My father could only see the upper half of the pony because of the crowd around the ring but what he saw pleased him and he bought it for 42gns, around £1,600 in today's money. He heard a few of the breeders sniggering and when he saw the horse close up he realised why. The Collier's front hooves were disfigured. They were so pigeon-toed they were unbelievable. As the saying goes, 'No foot, no horse!'

How was he to rectify this fault? My father started thinking and remembered a farrier who might be able to help. He took the animal immediately to Will Rhydybont, Llanybydder. Will inspected the pony and opined that it would take him three shoeings before he would succeed in straightening its hooves. He was absolutely right. Following Will's three shoeings, which would have taken place over a period of several months as the hooves grew, my father sold the collier at Llanybydder mart for 150gns, tripling his money. My father chose the right man for the job. His memory had come to the rescue.

After we moved to Crugybar our farriers were the Morgan family from Ffarmers, near Ffaldybrenin. They were father and son, Dai and later Eirian, professional singer Shân Cothi's father and brother respectively. Shân is a fine soloist and a popular radio and television presenter.

The presence of a good farrier can be all-important. At the Royal Welsh in 1983 I had already won the Cob championship, earning the right to go forward to the Supreme championship. But one of the mare's shoes was loose and so I called for Dai at Ffarmers. Over he came with his wife Joan, Eirian and Shân at 6.30 the following morning. It was critical that the shoe be replaced properly and as soon as possible. Thanks to their committed service the job was done in perfect time for us to be able to return to the show and compete in the Supreme championship.

After we moved to Pennant our farriers were Emlyn Lewis and his son Brian from Aberystwyth. These again were craftsmen of the highest order. Their smithy, in the middle of the town on Mill Street, was decked with photographs of shire horses they had shod over the years.

Some years ago I decided, for Myfanwy's birthday, to commission Emlyn to forge a brass horseshoe as a present for her. Bronze, apparently, is not an easy metal to work with, but Emlyn created a work of art and I composed a poetic couplet in Welsh to go with it:

> *Pedol aur ai graen yn glo*
> *Yw gwneud yn anrheg na a'n angho'*
> A golden shoe – its lustre locked
> Makes a never to be forgotten gift

The last horse I ever took to their Mill Street forge to be shod was Brynymor Welsh Magic, bred by a great character from

Talybont, D.J. Thomas, known as 'Tomos y Troi' (Thomas the Ploughman) from a mare bred by Rowlands of the Hwylog Stud. The shoes had been put on and I was ready to return home. As I led the horse out onto the street a Crosville bus thundered past so fast that Magic Bach was terrified and he jumped through the smithy window. Emlyn's diplomatic comment was, 'I needed a new window anyway!'

Luckily neither the horse nor anyone else were hurt. You'd never be allowed to have a smithy there nowadays, it was so close to the road. I believe it's a hairdresser's shop now.

Mr Lewis's bills were an artwork in themselves. We never like to get bills but his were so beautifully written out in copperplate that they were almost a pleasure to receive. He was also secretary of Aberystwyth show for many years and you could recognise when the show schedule arrived by the fine writing on the envelope.

Another blacksmith who attended to our horses was Cemaes Evans, who lived at Talsarn and later owned the Cathedine Stud at Brecon, after whom we used Huw Williams, Talsarn. During the latter years we have used Daniel Thomas, Gorsgoch, Llanybydder. Daniel's grandfather shod for my own grandfather, and Daniel's son, Rhodri, is following the same fine tradition, along with their apprentice Ioan Davies, Arthen Stud.

I would regularly visit the Anglesey show in the second week of August, arriving the night before after a long winding journey up the coast. One year I missed the show entrance. This was before the new road layout was constructed. It was 5.30 in the evening and the traffic was so heavy that it took me an hour-and-a-half to turn round and return.

The show announcer for years was Wil Huw, whose daughter Edna was once president and is still one of the chief officials. One year I showed Derwen Two Rivers in harness. I had named him for a special reason. I would rarely go outside the stud for new blood. I owned a horse called Rhystyd Flyer, bred by the Harris family of Mabwshen. A river ran through that area and this was also true of Crugybar. I envisaged the two rivers converging to give birth to this horse. He was a special horse and in harness was practically unbeatable.

At the Anglesey show the Ridden Cob class was about to start and our chief stable girl, Karin Fjeldbo, was on Derwen Two Rivers. She suddenly shouted, telling me that the horse had cast a shoe. This was an emergency, indeed a crisis. Sending it in on three shoes was impossible as it would severely affect the horse's balance.

I ran over to Wil Huw and told him I had a problem. He immediately called for the official show farrier on the tannoy, who within minutes came and shod the horse. Fortunately Derwen Two Rivers went on to win the class. I had been lucky. The farrier could have been busy elsewhere as he would always be on call. It was common for competitors to have their horses shod on site. One reason for this was that the service was free on show days!

Wil Huw was succeeded by Emyr Jones of the Esceifiog Stud. Nowadays the show announcer is Owen Griffiths of the Ilar Stud, grandson to the Davies Ffosbontbren family, Llanilar. All these announcers have had years of experience and create a unique atmosphere at the show with their commentaries.

In 2012 I was invited to address the Anglesey show annual dinner. The guest of honour was Prince William. As a result the chief executive of the society, Aled, was nicknamed 'Sir' Aled!

As for Two Rivers, I presented him to Karin when she left us to return home to Denmark at the beginning of the nineties. She, after all, had been responsible for breaking him in and training him. To all intents and purposes he was her horse.

In exactly the same way that as small eisteddfodau have nurtured the National Eisteddfod throughout the years, so many of the smaller country shows have fed into the Royal Welsh Show, forming a network of events that the Royal Welsh benefits from. One of the pinnacles of these contributing shows is the Lampeter Stallion Show, held nowadays at Talsarn, Ceredigion, on the third Saturday of April each year. The show is spearheaded by the chairman, John Green, Blaenplwyf, and his enlightened committee. This show is a dependable yardstick. Should an exhibitor's animal be successful here in April then it bodes well for them for the rest of the season. Other shows that we seldom miss include Rhandirmwyn and Cil-y-cwm and also Llangeitho. People like Chris, Walter, Eric, Meurig and many others form the backbone of such events. Without them there would be no future for the smaller shows nor, in turn, the Royal Welsh.

Ever since I started walking I have attended the Pontarddulais show, formerly with my parents, of course. From the very beginning I befriended a crew of fellow enthusiasts. Among them was Rhys Thomas, who, like me, attended Gelli Aur College. Then there was Roy Higgins and his brother Vernon from the Tireinion Stud. The show's chief executive was Gareth Courtney and it's great to know that he has been succeeded by his daughter Emma. Geraint the Auctioneer is another key figure, being the show announcer and the August Bank Holiday isn't complete unless I attend the Pontarddulais show.

One important decision accepted by the Society was to extend the Royal Welsh Show to four days. The campaign was led by Tudor Davies, Alan Turnbull and I, and in his book published on the Society's centenary, David W. Howell notes this. Looking back, it is great to see that the move has proved to be a resounding success. The Royal Welsh Show remains all important on the Welsh events calendar. A milestone was reached in 2013 with the retirement of chief executive David Walters following his highly successful 28 years at the helm. His successor Steve Hughson is already building on that success. An important development in the history of the Royal Welsh has been the establishment of the Winter Fair. The idea was first mooted by Tom Evans, Troedyraur, and at first there was no place for horses. I pleaded for their inclusion and the organisers' hand was forced in a critical year by the outbreak of foot-and-mouth disease, meaning that there was a ban on the movement of sheep and cattle. Horses have remained an integral part of the Fair ever since.

Llanddarog was the first show I ever judged and I think people were quite surprised when I put up Mrs Cuff's white Section B mare champion, Downland Jamila. Years later I selected her grandson Downland Jaguar to go to the Kulltorps Stud in Sweden, a country where he still lives, though now at the Arhults Stud, having been repatriated in 2017 to Ann Fishers' Mynyddgraig Stud in Surrey, so again a bloodline that stands the test of time. I've always had an interest in all the four sections of the Stud Book but we've never bred Section B's, although quite a few have passed through our hands. I was instrumental in securing the sale of the entire crop of nine foals from Downland in 2000, to be exported to Matts and Cecilia Olsson in Sweden. I had purchased the Downland Chevalier son, Paddock Carmargue, for them shortly after his Royal Welsh Male Championship in 1991. Casnewydd Showman by Sarnau Rheolwr was bought for Finland along with Polaris Jonquil who was Dyfed's pony here for a while. Interestingly Jonquil was out of Downland Jamila's sister, Downland Justina. We bred a few Section C's such as Derwen Dyfodol, who was by Rosina's Last and out of the Mountain Pony mare Derwen Dot by Clan Gylen. He was third at Lampeter Stallion Show as a yearling for the Saltmarsh Stud.

People say that I judge too quickly. I don't feel I judge quickly, I just try and do it efficiently. As soon as the class has been formed I start judging. I'll ask my steward to stop them and trot them up individually and I'll call them into line. I don't walk up and down the line as I'm going to see each animal out in front of me anyway. It's a matter of not wasting time. I was once at a forum for the Gwent Area Association and David Brake, Penycrug, was chairman. A gentleman stood up and said, 'Mr Chair, I would like to ask Ifor why I never see him touching the legs or checking the teeth or touching the horse at all. Why is that?' David turned to me to answer. 'It's very easy,' I said. 'Sometimes I have to decide if I'm buying a horse when I can't get closer than 20-30 yards to it, let alone feel its legs. And if, as I did, I managed to choose a wife in two minutes, why should I spend two hours looking at a horse?'

I remember one day at Llanybydder sale an acquaintance of my father came up to me and asked if we were entering Llandovery show that weekend, which was a good event in those days. Knowing that he was due to be the judge I replied that I believed we were planning on doing so, at which point he replied, 'Please don't!' I was a bit taken aback as I thought he liked our horse. His reply came back, 'It's not that I don't like your horse, but I owe "so-and-so" too much.' In an odd kind of way he was very honest as he didn't want to make a fool of himself, of me or of the horse!

I was rather thrown in the deep end when I deputised for my father at the Royal Welsh in 1974 as a very young person. It was quite an interesting job. I enjoyed it but perhaps if I did it again I'd have more confidence than I did aged 29. One amusing event at that show was in the three-year-old colt class. I saw this colt going around the ring and I thought to myself, 'That looks like a Derwen Cob.' So I called my steward over and asked him if he could check whether or not it was one with a Derwen prefix by looking in the catalogue. 'Yes,' he said, and confirmed it was Derwen Telynor! Nelson Smith had purchased him but didn't realise at that time that you couldn't show an animal under a judge that had bred or even had an interest in it. So Dick Swain was brought in to judge the class. It was just that 'Derwen look' that rang alarm bells with me, lucky I didn't proceed to judge him or I would have been in deep trouble. I was honoured to judge the Mountain Ponies in 1987 and then the Supreme Horse Championship in 2004.

In 1983 I was made an associate of the Royal Agricultural Societies in recognition of my work breeding and exporting Cobs, only to have this upgraded to a fellowship in 1988.

As well as the Welsh breeds I have also been honoured to judge for the Coloured Horse Society and the National Pony Society Mountain & Moorland panels. For the latter I was asked by the then chairman, Mrs Pat Campbell if as chairman of the WPCS. I would put myself forward for assessment. Apparently the NPS was continually getting lots of applications for Welsh breed judges, but few were on the NPS panel as many felt they didn't need to go forward for further assessment by another society, so it was felt that if the chairman was seen to be subjected to their scrutiny it might encourage other members to participate. Looking back the assessment must have been in the early 2000s at the Knowle Stud in Yorkshire.

They must have had 30 examples of the various native breeds to look at and judge with only eight of us applying for the Mountain & Moorland panel, and one very vocal person amongst us. Most of everybody, apart from myself, seemed to latch onto this vocal character. In came the animals and you had to write down the number and describe what you'd seen. This lovely bay animal came out and as I went up to its wither I could see it must have been about 15.1hh. I could hear the 'vocal' lady telling everybody what a lovely Connemara it was. Well even I knew that Connemaras don't come as big as 15.1hh – well, at least they shouldn't. So putting two and two together I realised that this must be some kind of trick and recognised it as a rather quality, rather fine but off-type Welsh Cob. So I wrote down my comments. The next animal was a New Forest, admittedly not what I would think was a very good New Forest but I could hear our 'vocal lady' telling everyone, 'No, it's not a New Forest, I breed them, I should know.' Then a plain Welsh Mountain two-year-old colt came forward with a very cresty neck and ridges on its feet, so again I wrote down my critical comments.

The assessment panel was chaired by the late Jenny Seymour, with Pat Campbell as the scribe, and when the time came for the first candidate to be interviewed nobody wanted to go in first, so I said to myself, 'Right, let's get on with this, I've got a long journey home,' and in I went.

Well, I started to give my reasons and had to apologise for talking against my own breed but I told them in no uncertain terms that the Mountain Pony was not a very good example!

'And on top of that I'm sure he's had laminitis by looking at his hooves,' I added. Jenny Seymour looked up and said, 'Mr Lloyd, if it's of any consolation to you, he's being gelded next week!' 'Thank goodness for that,' I replied. I went on to tell them that I could have been fooled by the big bay Welsh Cob, but thankfully for all of us the Fell Pony handler had a breed society badge and tie on so that helped us all, though on that day, I was the only one of the eight to get on, the rest had been misled by the 'vocal' character. It was like copying from somebody in an exam in school. If they're wrong, you're going to be wrong too.

It's very pleasing to see how the other native breeds have improved over time, for example the Highland Pony, which is no longer just depicted as the weight carrier which carries the stag of the moorland. They are prime examples of livestock improvement to me.

I think if members of the Welsh Pony and Cob Society continue to breed quality animals in all sections we have nothing to fear as far as popularity, but we do need to keep an eye over our shoulders as the other breeds are doing so well.

When I was assessed for the Coloured Horse & Pony panel we all went to the Endon Riding School and studied groups of animals, not necessarily coloured horses with the master judge, Nigel Hollings, before we went in front of the assessment panel. I can still remember a big bay riding school-type hunter of a horse with the biggest set of curbs on his hind legs. I asked how old he was only to find out he was 16 years old, so I imagined with all the hard work he would have had it was only to be expected that he was blemished. I went and sat down in front of the panel and the chairwoman, Caroline Hamilton, said to me, 'Well, Mr Lloyd, I'm afraid you've given us a serious problem.' This isn't boasting, it's a fact. 'What is the problem?' I asked. 'You've been awarded maximum marks,' she said. It was a good assessment and everybody learnt something that day.

We did export a beautiful grey New Forest stallion, Silverlea Snowstorm, to Finland who was very successful but I've never been tempted to keep anything other than the Welsh breeds.

I enjoy my trips away judging but following one stay at a bed and breakfast in Surrey I vowed that I would only stay away again in recognised hostelries or with close friends. I had arrived at a lovely Georgian redbrick farmhouse, complete with duck pond, which looked rather nice. Out came a lady with a clipboard and asked, 'Name?' I replied dutifully and she checked me off the list. 'Follow me,' she said and I turned towards the house. 'No, no, this way,' and we headed off to a row of wooden chicken sheds. This was where I was to sleep. They'd converted these sheds into bedrooms, I've never seen anything like it. It was a tiny room and the chair looked at least 100 years old, let alone the bed. They should have been reported, really, but I suppose that the lack of bed and breakfast facilities so close to Gatwick Airport means that rooms are at a premium. Another time I had been asked, last minute, to deputise for another judge at the Royal Cornwall show. Gwil Evans, Silian, came with me for a spin. The journey was horrendous as the A5 hadn't been extended at that time. We eventually arrived at the Palace Hotel in Newquay at about a quarter-to-nine, having left Aberaeron just after three. You can imagine that by the time we arrived in Cornwall we were absolutely exhausted, so I said to Gwil that we'd better go to the restaurant immediately as they would be closing at nine. We ordered our meal and I said to Gwil, 'Would you like a little bit of wine with that?' 'Yes,' he said. 'I rather fancy that Blue

Nun.' That was the only thing we could pronounce back in those days. Châteauneuf-du-Pape was a non-starter for us. The waiter brought the bottle to the table, along with a chit, a receipt. I said to him, 'What's this chit for?' He replied, 'The show society has instructed us to charge for all drinks this year.' 'Well, young man, it's nothing personal, but if I'm expected to pay for this bottle of plonk, having deputised, and then driven such a horrendous journey, I'm sorry but you'll have to tell the show that they'll need to find another deputy to judge tomorrow.' Ten minutes later, the waiter returned. 'That's quite alright, sir, the wine is on the house.' What had happened was that one of the previous year's cattle judges had run up a bar bill of £150, and we're talking 30 years ago, so he'd spoilt it for everyone.

The two stallions, Derwen Texas Express and Derwen Two Rivers, also competed in Long Distance Riding with Two Rivers qualifying for the Bronze Buckle award ridden by two of our Danish students. From my point of view it was one of the most boring jobs I have ever had to do. Sitting in the lorry, on top of the mountain, waiting for hours and hours and hours for them to come back! Derwen Rondevous (Derwen Quartz x Derwen Repartee by Derwen Replica), also known as 'Rodney', and his Paralympic dressage rider Sophie Wells were bronze medal winners and highest British Team member in Belgium 2005, amongst many national victories that laid the foundation for more international success. She was awarded an MBE in the 2013 New Year's Honours list for services to equestrianism. 'Rodney' was originally sold to the Proctor family from Preston who put in his basic training, before he formed a fantastic partnership with Sophie who purchased him as a ten-year-old via the internet. 'He turned out to be a very special person,' says Sophie. 'He took me from novice to advanced medium in no time. We have a good partnership – we like and respect each other. He might not have been the most traditional dressage horse but he taught me so much. I competed up to Prix St. George and trained all the Grand Prix movements. He had so much character.' A glowing recommendation for the Welsh Cob. Sophie was awarded Equestrienne of the Year at the Horse of the Year Show in 2017.

In 1983 we were presented to Her Majesty the Queen in the main ring at the Royal Welsh as we were Champion that year with Derwen Princess. My father had met her at the 1955 Royal Welsh Bicentenary Show in Brecon with the original foundation mare Dewi Rosina who had won both in-hand and under saddle that year. I don't think she remembered. The Duke of Edinburgh showed a lot of interest in Princess's shoeing as I remember. Funnily enough, some years later I was introduced to the Princess Royal at the Three Counties Show with Derwen Groten Goch the year she qualified for the Lloyds Bank final at the Horse of the Year Show. I did say to her that I'd had the honour of meeting her mother a few years previously. 'Ah yes,' she replied, 'but you had a black mare then didn't you?' So somebody must have been doing their homework.

In 2001 a unique venture was launched at Aberaeron. The idea for the Welsh Cob Festival was the brainchild of Clive Hoyles of the Llangybi Stud who had visited a horse festival at Golega in Portugal. The festival, held on the Square Field at Aberaeron, is by now well established attracting over 3,000 visitors annually to the town and some 100 horses. In 2005, to commemorate the Society's centenary a full-sized bronze statue of a Welsh Cob was unveiled nearby on Alban Square opposite the Feathers Hotel. Its sculptor was David Mayer.

When the idea was mooted we feared that we could never afford to commission such an ambitious statue. David, having previously sculpted a statue of Derwen Quartz for the 2004 Royal Welsh Show, was a friend and I discussed the idea with him. David's incredible gesture was to do the work for free, charging only for materials, which was an extremely kind gesture. To celebrate the unveiling, poet Dic Jones wrote a Welsh verse. In it he described the Cob as the star among European horses. He described their four silver hooves, lively as mercury ending with the statement that three Cs, not four, owned the land. Yes, the Three Cs, the horseshoe-shaped letters in this case being Cymdeithas Cobiau Cymru (The Welsh Pony and Cob Society). But they also echoed my Three Cs, Concerts, Car and Cobs. Yes, without a doubt, the Three Cs own this land.

GARTH VILLA 1947

Chapter Five

Changing times
'The Parliament is in London, the Cob is here.'

My mother was supremely organised in whatever she undertook in-between raising us and running the house and jobs on the farm. This snapshot of the diaries she kept gives us an insight of how life was nearly 80 years ago:

1947 Diary of Elin Lloyd
January
1st – 20-25 children called to wish us all a happy
new year.
2nd – Sold Rosie's colt for £25 and Megan's for £15-0-0.
5th – Maggie from Manorafon here, played with Ifor, 'I spy
with my little eye' after supper.
18th – Salting the pig and churning, Roscoe at Lampeter car
mart. Cars very dear, offered a man at Pencader £300 for
a 1937 Austin 10. He had been offered £500, so he said!
24th – Had a very enjoyable evening played darts and Tit-bit.
29th – Coldest day for 66 years.
30th – Llanybydder. Roscoe trimming mare ready for the mart,

also trimming another horse and pony. Sold horse for
£35 then the buyer sold him again for £6 loss. Very poor
trade, buyers could not get down. Smallest mart for years.

February

2nd – Very heavy fall of snow, 8-9 inches deep on the road.
Took photos with camera of Dewi Rosina. No milk lorry.

18th – Sheep and ponies on the mountains are freezing to death
by the hundreds.

25th – Started snowing heavily about seven o'clock.

27th – Horse sale at Llanybydder. Good few horses there
considering the weather.

28th – Very hard frost, snow still on the ground.

March

1st – Roscoe and Ifor at home, they listened to a very good St
David's Day programme on the radio.

4th – Very cold, hard frost. Went to Llandysul. Bought a
pair of rubber boots for Ifor 12/6 *(shillings)*. Started for
home straight away as it was beginning to snow, went as
far as just above Blaencwm Pen Top. Got stuck on the
hill behind a row of cars. Then managed to reverse to
Blaencwm. Mrs Jones persuaded us to stay the night.

5th – We slept at Blaencwm. Lucky they had room enough to
put us up. Roscoe and Jones walked through the drifts to
Llanfihangel to get news to home.

6th – The blizzards eased about 7 o'clock. Slept night in
Blaencwm, a restful night after we got to know that all
was well at home. We trekked down to the village to see
for a train. No train. We went back to Blaencwm and

slept another night. They welcomed us back heartily. A home from home. They were kindness itself.

7th – 10 o'clock we started walking down to Llanfihangel. Got down to the station about 11 o'clock just in time to catch the train. Got into Llanybydder, got a cordial welcome home and then we walked to Garth.

8th – Well, started work with a vengeance. Put 5 gallons of milk ready. Boys clearing Cefnrhyddlan ready for tractor to go through to get the milk to Llanybydder.

10th – Milk lorry collecting again.

11th – Up early. Roscoe and the boys took the tractor to Blaencwm. Got both cars back home.

14th – Art, Glen, Roscoe and self to Lampeter Furniture sale. Good furniture. Bought a lovely dresser £28-5-0. Glen bought a bedroom suite £55.00.

20th – Evan's birthday. Made trifle and sponges and iced cake. Had a nice birthday tea.

28th – Took chestnut Cob to Llanybydder. Sold for £80-0-0 to Mr Billingsley of Warwickshire. He and his friend and Osborne-Jones came for tea. Alfie sold a beautiful mare for £57-0-0 to some people from Pontarddulais. Much too cheap.

April

11th – Roscoe sold tractor and plough for £38-0-0. Good work.

12th – Miss Garton and I caught the 7.30am train to Ammanford. *(Miss Garton came as a teacher during the War from Liverpool to Wales with evacuee children. She stayed with us at Garth Villa for several years.)*

19th – Haydn here. Evan, he, Ifor and Ronald to Llanybydder
with Dewi Rosina (Rosie) in trap.

23rd – Lampeter races had to be postponed owing to bad
weather. Roscoe in the morning to see about a horse but
no good. Self baking sponges and cakes.

24th – Off early all of us to Llanybydder Horse Sale. Top price
for us £162-0-0. Colliers £167-0-0. Osbourne-Jones and
Blackwell back here for tea, then we went to Pentrebrain
(home of Pentre Eiddwen Comet) bought filly foal.

25th – Roscoe and I off to Llanybydder 2/3y.o sale. He bid
£31-0-0 for a rising two-year-old Cob. Helped an old
fellow from Penuwch to sell a yearling Cob for £31-0-0.
Roscoe, Ifor and I to Pencader to see the new David
Brown Tractor man. Would not sell but came to terms to
hire for 6 months.

27th – Roscoe, Evan, Ifor and self to Pentrefelin to visit Mam.
Mam up in gegin *(kitchen)* and feeling better but still
weak, nice to see her downstairs. Ifor & Dilys there as
well. *(Ifor was Elin's brother.)*

May

15th – Self fetched rations from shop.

29th – Horse sale at Llanybydder. Artie sold 2.y.o. filly for
£35-0-0 to his brother in law and bought a good mare
from W.Jones, Neuaddfawr for £53-0-0.

31st – Roscoe, Brook, Ifor, Evan and I to football match final at
Lampeter. Aberaeron won 2 – Nil.

June

12th – Sennybridge Horse sale. Roscoe bought a lovely little
pony for Ifor named 'Snowflake' - £28

August

5th – Packing Roscoe off to Royal Welsh. Self cooking.

6th – Up at 4.30am to do the milking then off to Royal Welsh
Show, Carmarthen. Ifor at Glynfaes. Roscoe came 2nd and
Reserve Champion Female. Made dozens of cups of tea.

7th – Maggie, Brook, Ifor and Self to Royal Welsh. Roscoe took
2nd prize for mare and foal. Should have had 1st. We all
stayed at Carmarthen. Slept in the box. *(Straw hotel)*

8th – Last day of Royal Welsh.

15th – Mr & Mrs Felix called to see Dewi Rosina. Roscoe bought
her from Mr Felix.

20th – Aberystwyth Agricultural Show – Dewi Rosina (Rosie)
took the Loxdale Cup and 2nd Under Saddle.

September

3rd – Drefach Show. Roscoe had 1st in Welsh Cob class, 2nd
Under Saddle and Reserve Champion. Seren y Garth 1st
yearling class. Brenin Cledlyn was 2nd in sucker class.
Pansy 1st in 3y.o. class. Self won 1st prize Plum jam, Ifor 3rd
with his kidney beans.

10th – Llangwyryfon Show. Dewi Rosina 1st in her class and
Champion. Yearling filly won 1st and Snowflake 2nd.

19th – Lampeter Show. Grand success. Dewi Rosina took first
prize in Welsh Cob class and also the medal and J.T.
Morgan Silver Cup.

25th – Sold Ifor's white pony Snowflake for £41-0-0. Paid £28-0-0 for her.

27th – My birthday.

28th – Evan, Ifor and I went down to Pentrefelin. Had nice afternoon. Ifor and I picked apples in orchard. Went to 'Shed y Gwenyn *(honey bee shed)*, brought back memories of 'nhad' *('my father')*. Evan drove car through the river and we called at Brynaeron. *(Ifor, Elin's brother lived there.)*

October

3rd – Very busy day. Morning getting ready to meet buyers from Birmingham to buy. Gwenog Tulip, 3y.o. sold for £150-0-0, real good price. Her sister Marie sold for £85-0-0. Their mother, Daisy Gwenog was bought for £70-0-0 and then sold for £150-0-0. If every animal paid like Daisy farming would be worthwhile.

4th – Bought 15 hens at 9/- *(shillings)* each.

16th – Roscoe and I to Llwynffynnon sale. Bought cow £33-0-0. Horse £45-0-0. Bought young sow £28-0-0.

18th – Roscoe went to Pengolgau sale. He bought eleven ewes and one ram. 6 @ 26/- and 5 @ 27/-. Self bought a heifer for £21-0-0, first I've bought in my life. Hope it turns out trumps!

November

20th – Ifor to school tea party. Sang on his own for the first time in public. *(Aged four.)*

22nd – Pentrebrain and Pantyblawd here to see a horse. Did not buy.

December

3rd – Went to sale in Llanybydder. Bought toy cart horse for Ifor's Christmas stocking and a photo frame to put the black Cob in.

13th – Uncle Rhys here cleaning the chimney ready for Santa Claus for Ifor. Made sponge cakes and flans in new tins.

16th – Lampeter Mart – Cows selling well. Three over £100.

18th – Self busy. Made Ifor's birthday cake ready for the 27th. Also made eight Christmas puddings. Good job done.

24th – Roscoe and self to Pentrefelin to see Mam. Wonderfully well. Took sponges and cakes.

25th – Like Spring in the morning. Spent Christmas at home. Had lovely dinner together. Roscoe's birthday.

27th – Ifor's birthday. Had a grand party at home and good fun.

With Mam being a member of the Pentrefelin family, it was no surprise that she had bardic traits. She once composed a rhyme that summarised the needs of a Welsh Cob:

> On the level, never spare me,
> On the hill, don't ever force me,
> On the decline do not ride me,
> In the stable don't ignore me.

She wasn't without her promotional streak, either, when in 1968 she wrote to Buckingham Palace to see if Prince Charles would care to come to Ynyshir to ride a Cob when he was at University in Aberystwyth. She even offered him Derwen Groten Ddu who was considered 'the best riding mare'. She did have a reply from the prince's private secretary Sqdn. Ldr. David Checketts who wrote, 'Naturally the Prince has no idea of how much time he will have at Aberystwyth, particularly as this will be just before the investiture, however your offer will be kept in mind.' Unfortunately the Prince never found time, but Mam and Groten Ddu made it into the *Western Mail.*

Referring to Prince Charles reminds me of a visit he and Princess Diana made to Cardigan in 1981. Prior to their arrival, teams of detectives and dogs had been combing the town for any explosives that could have been hidden. Every manhole was raised and drains searched. What the officers were unaware of was that there was a fellow living in the town who had enough explosives to blow Cardigan sky high. He was Tom Powell, known locally as 'Tom the Bomb'. He was an explosives expert employed by the county council and held a special permit.

Following Mam's death in 1992, Myfanwy and I began clearing the house. It was a difficult task as time and again something would trigger off a memory and uncover old reminiscences, drawing me back to the past. Suddenly I remembered the gold medals father had won at Mydroilyn in 1923-24. There was no trace of them anywhere. I feared that they had been discarded, thrown out among the lumber and lost forever. Myfanwy, however, was determined not to give up the search. She looked meticulously through all the discarded dross once again. She even searched through a jumble of Mam's old shoes that were to be thrown out. She pushed her hand into the toe of a shoe and there she found the medals. What made her choose that particular shoe? She still can't explain why, and so I had one medal, my brother Ifan had the other. Ifan died in the autumn of 2016.

The changes I have witnessed in the countryside during my life have been astounding. When I was a child practically everyone in the Crugybar neighbourhood spoke Welsh. Even those families that moved in, including us, were Welsh-speakers. But I well remember a pair of English incomers taking over the Royal Oak in Pumpsaint towards the end of the fifties. Typically, my parents welcomed Mr and Mrs McClinton with open arms. Originally from the north of England, their northern accent was difficult to follow. But they became such close friends of the family that Ifan and I always referred to them as Uncle Frank and Aunty Lil.

Aunty Lil took great pride in her expertise in brewing tea. She considered the Welsh as barbarians as far as brewing tea was concerned. She always parked a massive teapot on the Aga. She would never empty that teapot. Every time the tea ran out she would add more spoonfuls and pour boiling water over both the fresh leaves and the lees. That meant that her tea was the colour of treacle and almost as thick.

My father was also my mentor during his life. His love of singing rubbed off on me. He entrusted in me the secrets of breeding cobs and selling and buying cars and indeed horses. He passed away, aged 80, on the 13th June 1983.

He had proved himself in all he undertook and I would have been a fool not to have followed his example. One piece of advice he offered to me, one that I will always remember, is not to give anyone more than one chance. Should anyone do you a bad turn, you should never give that person the opportunity of doing so again. That was his philosophy. In other words, you should learn from your mistakes rather than repeat them. If someone manages to make a fool of you once, he or she will do it again if given the chance.

My philosophy therefore is, 'One strike and you're out'. And it has served me well throughout my life. It is not an easy philosophy to follow. But it is my golden rule and I have had no regrets in adhering to it. Life is too short for regrets.

Soon after I took over the garage business I was persuaded to stand for election for the town council. I was duly elected. I was only 20 years old, the youngest ever Aberaeron town councillor. I wasn't tempted to go any further in local government. My paternal grandfather had been a county councillor and this indirectly led to him losing everything. He and his fellow councillors, prior to meetings at the town, would gather at the Feathers Hotel for a meal. Many of the town's business people would join them there. My grandfather was one of Nat West's first customers when it opened a branch in town. A new manager was appointed at the bank and he and grandfather met at the Feathers. Grandfather happened to tell him that he had a sum of money to pay in. The manager suggested he accept the money and would deposit it in grandfather's account. This became standard practice, a monthly ritual. But several months later, grandfather realised that not one penny had been paid into his bank account. He lost everything and the bank manager conveniently disappeared.

I learnt a lot through being a town councillor. I was now shoulder to shoulder with the business and community leaders of the town, people such as Hughes Jones the Butcher, Mr Thomas the Headmaster, that great character Vic Hubbard and Mrs Sewell, who became notorious. She must have owned half the town buying houses and renting them out.

Considering that my maternal grandfather, Dan Jenkins, Pentrefelin, was one of the founders of the Welsh Pony and Cob Society back in 1901 it was only natural that I should become a member early in life, 1967 to be exact. I was honoured to become its seventh ever chairman in 1997 and president in 2017. In the sixties, seventies and eighties the general meetings were often held at Shrewsbury. The reason for this was that Lord Kenyon, the then longstanding chairman (1962-1990), lived nearby at Whitchurch. The headquarters were at Aberystwyth, ably administrated by Tom Roberts with Pam Hutchins (later Evans) and Llinos Spencer assisting. The headquarters is now in the Aeron Valley on the site of what used to be a centre for disabled children between Felinfach and Aberaeron.

The Society meetings were held bi-monthly and I would drive over to Shrewsbury with J.H. Davies, Bigni, of the Valiant Stud, Pauline Taylor from the Llanarth Stud and Mrs Cuff from the Downland Stud. Once, just outside Newtown, I was stopped by the police for speeding. But I had friends in high places and I did not hear anything further on the matter. It was, however, a lesson worth learning. No doubt we were in the middle of a heated discussion and I wasn't paying attention to the speedometer. I took more care afterwards.

At the beginning of the seventies, shortly after I joined the Welsh Pony and Cob Society a new constitution was put forward for acceptance. One of the most contentious proposals was a clause that demanded the Society's headquarters be situated in England or Wales. It was my mother who drew attention to this anomaly and she urged me to raise the matter. My mother was strongly in favour of the headquarters being situated in Wales and nowhere else. Naturally, I agreed with her.

Off I went to the meeting, and accompanying me in the car was my father and Mr Amos and his daughter Linda from the Redwood Stud. At the meeting Lord Kenyon proposed that the new constitution should be accepted *en bloc*. I proposed the amendment that one particular clause, the second on the list, should be changed to demand that the Society's headquarters should be situated in Wales and nowhere else. Lord Kenyon almost swallowed his spectacles! He wasn't used to any opposition. Accepting the amendment, he insisted, would mean postponing the publishing of the new constitution. I stood up again and formally proposed the amendment. And although I hadn't canvassed other members, the amendment was carried.

Following my success at that meeting a group of members, led by Don Edwards of the Minsterly Stud, urged me to stand as a prospective member of the Society's council. I stood and was elected, serving from 1971 until 2005. I was then further honoured by being made a Fellow of the Royal of England Agricultural Society as an appreciation of my contribution to the agricultural industry. I was nominated on account of the history and success of the Derwen Stud, recorded in writing. The honour meant that I was being acknowledged by all member countries in the UK. And further to this, in 2001, the Welsh Pony and Cob's centenary year, I was voted chairman, the first Welshman ever to be honoured in such a way. As part of the centenary celebrations, Shân Legg-Bourke from the Glanusk estate organised a very successful photographic exhibition of horse portraits.

Not everything went smoothly, however. In fact I put the cat among the pigeons by demanding an internal inquiry into the Welsh Pony and Cob Society's accounts. There were occasional inquiries but they were not held as regularly as I wished. A regular check would ensure that no error or oversight would be possible regarding payments received by members for their horse sales and subsequent transfer of ownership. Should I own a hundred horses that meant I was to have made a hundred payments? There were some objections, one being the impossibility of inspecting the accounts of seven or eight thousand members. I accepted that argument but demanded that we, the Council members' accounts should be examined as examples for the purpose of transparency.

My request seemed totally harmless on the surface. But obviously I had inadvertently disturbed a hornet's nest. I must have struck a nerve somewhere as it led to a small caucus attempting to blacken my character. The dissension persisted for some length of time. Some of the insinuations used against me were obviously libellous. Indeed this was obviously clear when two members appeared on television slandering me. I was left with no alternative but to seek legal advice. A barrister I counselled with was of the opinion that I, as a man in the public eye, could demand substantial compensation that could bankrupt both members. I, however, settled for the notional compensation sum of just one pound and a public apology. Myfanwy and I felt that had I accepted full compensation I would only be taking money from the members. This would mean punishing innocent parties as well as the slanderers. The cheque for that one pound remains uncashed. But my good character remains intact.

There is an element in eisteddfod circles that is known as 'cythraul canu', meaning 'the demon of song'. It involves underhanded rivalry. I believe that the demon of the horse world also exists. This episode also demonstrated the truth of an old adage that claims that a Welshman's greatest enemy is always another Welshman, and it's sad to have to say that most of those who tried to slander and libel me were themselves Welsh. But the cruellest slight of all was to accuse me of deceit, a totally false claim. Some even went as far as to complain to the Charities Commission with their totally fraudulent accusation.

The Commission's accountants went through my books with a fine tooth comb without coming up with any attempt to falsify as much as one entry, either deliberately or by accident. They found that I had entered every transaction and had done so correctly. Furthermore, during my five-year tenure as chairman I desisted from showing even one of my horses so as to dispel any accusation of favouritism by any judge.

No, there was no basis for any complaint and I accepted the one pound compensation, a symbolic token of my total innocence. But much more important than any compensation, even if I had been awarded a million pounds, was the public apology in the form of a letter. It appeared in the local paper, the *Cambrian News* that circulates widely throughout West, Mid and North Wales. It appeared on 24th March 2005 and I quote it in full below:

> *'The Welsh Pony and Cob Society, 6 Chalybeate Street, Aberystwyth, SY23 1HB statement: The Welsh Pony and Cob Society is pleased to announce that the long-running dispute with Council Member Mr I.J.R. Lloyd has been resolved. After a thorough investigation in which Mr I.J.R. Lloyd co-operated fully, it has been irrefutably established that there were no fraudulent claims against the Society's funds by him. The Council wishes it to be known that the views expressed on television were personal views only. The matter is now closed and no further action will be taken by either side.'*

I was cleared completely but I still feel bitter about the matter. Should I be blamed for that? Shortly after the dispute, two of my accusers were found guilty of various offences. Yes, as the hymn goes, God works in mysterious ways.

There were, though, plenty of high points during my time as chairman. I've always been a big believer in publicity. Towards the end of the seventies, during the filming of the television programme by the name of *Cob Country*, I was asked on camera to explain the characteristics of the Welsh Cob. I was asked why Cardiganshire was known as the Land of the Cobs. My answer was simple. 'It is like this: the Parliament is in London, the Cob is here.'

Any publicity for Welsh Cobs and Welsh Mountain Ponies is to be welcomed, and one excellent idea was put forward by the society secretary, Evelyn Jones. She joined the staff having previously been secretary of the Welsh Black Cattle Society. Evelyn came up with the idea of presenting a pony to Dylan, son of Hollywood stars Catherine Zeta Jones and Michael Douglas.

The Council first approached Dai Jones, Catherine's father from Swansea. He took to the idea immediately. We then looked for the calmest Mountain Pony we could find by contacting all our members. Few decided to answer but we found a perfect animal through one of our members, Mrs Kathleen James and her husband Colin at the Highland Stud in Sussex. She sold it to the Society at a most reasonably reduced price. He measured 11.2 hands and was named Highland Jinx. We arranged to present the pony personally to Catherine in Cardiff. It cost us £10,000 to transport the pony to her and Michael's ranch in Arizona.

When Evelyn phoned Catherine in Los Angeles she asked the actress whether she had a large garden. She couldn't fathom what Evelyn was on about. But when she realised the significance of the question she was delighted with the idea as she loved horses, and her garden, of course, was large enough. This meant a new departure for the Society as the only celebrities to be presented with Cobs or Ponies previously were members of the Royal Family. The idea worked like a dream with the Society receiving worldwide publicity.

Another success was a very innovative idea put forward by Myfanwy. She suggested electing an honorary young ambassador for the society on an annual basis. A trophy was designed and fashioned by Robin Upton of Ciliau Aeron, who specialises in restoring oak furniture. The stained glass work as part of the design was carried out by Richard Molineux from Middlesex, the son of my cousin Ann. The glass panel was modelled in national colours with a rearing image of Derwen Replica. That first year some 24 applicants offered themselves up for consideration. The first to be chosen as Ambassador was Phillipa Aitken from Scotland, a keen exhibitor of Section B ponies. Among those chosen later was a local man, Owen Griffiths from the Ilar Stud, Llanilar. The current Young Ambassador is Euros Llŷr Morgan of the Cwmtawe Stud, who has not only been an incredibly enthusiastic recipient but has also become an invaluable help to us here on the stud.

The most interesting aspect of being Chair was meeting people. I took the time to go around the area associations to let them know how much their contribution and their work was appreciated. I don't think any previous Chair had done that.

I was invited up to Scotland by Gladys Dale to address their association. By the time we returned to her home, The Pillars, on the edge of the coastline, there was no electricity in the house due to the terrible storms. Gladys was going around on her hands and knees in the dark looking for the whisky bottle and the glasses and all I could see were the ships sailing out at sea by the light of the night. There were terrible floods that night, so all the return trains had been cancelled. But I had to get back, so we went into Newcastle to try and rent a car. All that was available was a Fiat Punto, which wasn't going to be available until 4.30pm so I had no choice. By the time I passed the Angel of the North it was about 4.45pm and I managed to dodge the worst of the weather to get as far as Machynlleth, where I could see a lorry ahead of me submerged in water. Thankfully we had good friends, Gwyn and Evelyn, who lived locally so I was able to turn around and seek them out, their response being, 'It's taken a flood for you to visit us at last?' Luckily they had a 4x4 which I followed via a back road over the hill to Talybont. The problem was that everyone had the same idea on this narrow lane, going in both directions, including buses so it was absolute chaos but I eventually managed to get home by midnight.

The staff at the office were always helpful. I remember when Derwen Revelation was three I couldn't find his registration certificate. I rang the WPCS office and spoke to Pam, who said she would look him up in case it had been mislaid somewhere. She rang me back later and said, 'I'm sorry, Ifor, he's not registered. You've filled in the Birth Notification Form but you haven't transferred it to full registration.' Both his sire's parents had to be blood-typed, as well as himself, and then the late penalty fee on top of that – it was an expensive registration. The irony was that I was the one who proposed the adoption of this evidence-based form of registration, as every year we had sob stories from people who had forgotten to complete their forms before the end of year deadline. Following the testing at that time Nebo Black Magic,

Derwen Llwynog, Rosina's Last and True To Forms, I think, were the only Cob stallions at stud of proven parentage.

Although Myfanwy and I took over the stud following our marriage, the garage business continued, taking up much of our time. In 1985 we decided to give up the garage business entirely and concentrate on running the stud, the only other business we knew anything about. We decided to revert to my father's way of life during the 1940s, buying and selling Cobs. The Cobs had been around throughout my life. But now we decided to really go for it.

I once said to a friend, 'There's a difference between you and me.' 'What's that?' he replied. 'Is it that I am taller than you? 'No, no,' I said. 'The difference is that the horses are a hobby for you. I've had to make a living out of mine.' 'I hadn't thought about that, but you're right, it's a fact,' he said.

When our son Dyfed was born in 1981, our world was complete. He attended Pennant School where Beti Griffiths was headmistress. Beti, then Williams, and I attended Crugybar School together. Dyfed went on to Aberaeron Comprehensive School where Marina James was the headteacher, and she and her staff were brilliant. Dyfed was successful in 11 GCSE subjects and was especially fortunate in his computer studies teacher, Dai Lloyd. Dyfed loved computer studies.

He also inherited my interest in Welsh Cobs. He began competing in shows in both in-hand and under saddle sections, initially with the Mountain Ponies and then the Cobs. He enjoyed no little success, but the computing took priority. Unfortunately it's a subject that holds no appeal to me.

Dyfed's sixth-form studies took him to Llandovery College. He stayed with his grandparents. He then heard that Stafford

University had a good reputation in computer studies and enrolled there. I was delighted in his choice of subject as it was a commercially-focused course. Too many young people today are attracted to courses that turn out to be meaningless to them later in life, leaving them unemployable. It resulted in him gaining employment after his degree. After seven years with the television production company Tinopolis, Dyfed joined a computer firm in Swansea, though has now returned to Tinopolis, based in Llanelli.

Cobs have always been an important part of my life, not only as a business but even more importantly as an integral part of the local community. For years it was a tradition that I would travel around the district every New Year's Eve with horse and cart to wish the neighbours a Happy New Year. We owned a cob, Rhystyd Flyer, born at the Rhystyd Stud. This cob again was descended from the original black mare, Dewi Rosina. At the time we had a stable girl called Sheila from Dorset working with us. She was rather straight-laced in her ways. Later she and her husband went on to oversee one of Princess Anne's farms. However one New Year's morning I arrived at Tŷ Coch, Pennant, where a lady, Marged Ann lived. She offered Sheila a drop of wine, which was accepted. Marged Ann went to the kitchen and returned with a full bottle of whisky and two glasses. She filled both glasses and Sheila and I gulped them down and away we went with the horse and cart. By the time we were halfway to Cross Inn, Sheila's tongue had miraculously been loosened and out came the most risqué of stories. Yes, that was quite a start to the New Year!

Every Christmas I would carry Father Christmas around the neighbourhood in our horse and cart on behalf of the local nursery school. Reg Jones would be Santa and by the time I would pick him up at Rhos yr Hafod pub, the celebrations would already be well advanced. One Christmas with Reg having clambered onto the cart I gave the horse a light touch with the whip. Rather than just quicken its pace, the horse started galloping. It was bedlam. As we came to an abrupt stop by the school, Santa fell out of the cart. He got up groggily and made a promise, 'That's the last time I'll ever come with you in the cart again!' I think he stuck to reindeer and a sleigh from then on.

I like to think that we as a family, and our Cobs, were a natural part of the community. Today that community is part of the larger world. Myfanwy came up with the idea of organising courses for those who were interested in keeping Cobs but who had no previous experience. Cob breeders, like their horses, are usually part of a lineage going back generations. Indeed, the experienced breeders' lineage is just as important as that of their cobs. This can make it difficult for outsiders who are new to the breed to gain admittance and be accepted.

Some twelve years ago we therefore began organising weekend courses for newcomers into the world of Cobs. This made it possible for them to be immersed in Cob culture, including taming colts, saddling, handling and showing as well as learning how to choose a Cob. We covered every aspect. These courses became very popular and as far as we know they were the only courses of their kind in the world. We attracted some 20 or more enthusiasts every three or four months.

In 2009 we decided to sell off most of the farm machinery. With only Myfanwy and I living on the farm, and our decision to concentrate on the Cobs, we had no need for most of the implements. I am often asked why Dyfed isn't part of the business. The truth of the matter is that I could never afford to pay him the wages he earns from his computing expertise. He lives and works in a totally different world to the one I was part of when I was in my early thirties. And it's high time that we all admitted that those days are gone, never to return. We are too inclined to look back rather than forward.

Chapter Six

The Future
'When I look for a Mountain Pony I want to find a type of pony that I can put a child on his back and fly away.'

I'm quite a magpie as a collector of eisteddfod and Cob trivia and memorabilia. I have already mentioned my autograph book and my trophies. Over the years I have also collected dozens of sale catalogues and concert programmes as well as relevant newspaper cuttings. I can still recall the registration numbers of leading animals in the Welsh Stud Book. One of my weaknesses, though, is my complete lack of orderliness. Luckily I have a wife who is the complete opposite. I couldn't do anything without Myfanwy! She is a paragon of neatness and she has filed all my memorabilia. I hardly throw anything away. Mam was the same and Myfanwy has the same tendency. I consider such a habit as a virtue. People tend to be too ready to discard things. Documents and photographs are thrown away regardless of their future importance. But, thanks to Mam, I have always been reluctant to discard anything that might prove to be of interest in the future. We have albums and scrapbooks piled high here, many of which should perhaps move to the next level and be scanned into a digital format for posterity.

The decision to set up a museum here on the farm was Myfanwy's back in 1994. We had a lot of artefacts at Ynyshir and several friends and family who were interested in farming history donated items. The main things were horsey and farm items; and it grew from there. We used to be open to the public for several years but what we do now is to show it off as part of our heritage to groups of enthusiasts that may visit.

Over the years, students from all over the globe have come to us for work experience. Most have been from the UK, having been sent here by Mina Davies Morrell, a lecturer at Aberystwyth University. As well as gaining valuable veterinary experience, those from abroad have also been able to learn or polish their English, thanks to Myfanwy. This is an important element in our curriculum, with Myfanwy teaching them basic words and phrases before expanding the spectrum.

A neighbour of ours at Aberarth, Inga from Russia who married a local man, is now fluent in Welsh following Myfanwy's tutorials. This she managed within two years. She loves horses and comes here regularly to go out riding. She began receiving Welsh lessons every Sunday morning. She now speaks six languages, Welsh being the latest.

Those students who have spent time with us over the years have become emissaries by taking the name of Derwen Stud with them all over the world. At one time our students, staying for a year, would be able to study for their NVQ. I would also teach them skills such as leading and saddling horses, and Myfanwy would teach them stable management. This would be done in conjunction with Coleg Ceredigion and the British Horse Society.

Some would go on to study at university. Nowadays we accept just one or two for a few weeks at a time.

These students are most grateful to us but we are just as grateful to them for spreading the word about our stud in their home countries. This ensures worldwide publicity for us. In fact they bring the world to our stud and then take us back home with them all over the globe.

We remained a British Horse Society approved training establishment for nearly 25 years, which meant they could do a 'spot check' at any time. Major Hill, who was the regional co-ordinator, did tell Myfanwy once that if everywhere he visited was like the Derwen Stud he'd soon be out of a job. Standards had to be kept high, right down to the students not being allowed to wear blue jeans on the yard. We've relaxed that rule today.

One of the best grooms we ever had here was Sheila French, who remained with us for three years. Sheila could always be relied upon to be in the right place at the right time. At a show, there was none better. So much so that when she left we offered her the pick of the colt foals to start up her own stud in Hampshire. She chose Derwen Teithiwr (Derwen Adventure Boy x Derwen Telynores) who she had great success with. However, we're reminded of her time here daily as she introduced her mother, the renowned sculptress, Irene French to Derwen Replica. Irene will only sculpt a horse that she is inspired by and at that point the only other horses she had modelled were the Arabian stallion Haroun and a copy of the Ferrari rearing horse for racing driver Nigel Mansell. Her statue of Replica fills us both with pride and pleasure each day.

The internet is a very important factor these days. Technology has made the world so much smaller. I remember buying my first mobile phone back in 1985. Today they are referred to as pocket phones. At that time, mobile phones were too big and clumsy to fit in anyone's pocket. A couple from England, Paul Taylor and Stephanie Edwards, came here to buy a few Cobs. I had only just bought my mobile phone to be placed in the lorry. Paul worked in telecommunications with the Royal Mail and was well-versed in modern technology. I remember him prophesying that within a few years, mobile phones would be as small as a Mars Bar. I laughed cynically at the time. But he was right. Nowadays they are almost as small as After Eight chocolates!

I shall always remember when we were little children in primary school there was a map of the world on the wall with the British Empire marked in red, plastered all over the map. I suggested to the Welsh Pony and Cob Society Council that we should seek to do something similar, showing where the Welsh breeds had found themselves. They laughed, saying all the world knows about the Welsh breeds. I said no. The proof of the matter was that when the weather was bad, Charlie Pollak of the Caeiago trekking centre near Llanwrda would send guests over to Derwen to look at Cobs and the museum in the dry. I well remember a group of American servicemen and their families coming over here, just your general 'Joe Bloggs' horse riders. I remember asking them, 'Before you came to Caeiago, how many of you had heard of Mountain Ponies?' Not one hand went up. I asked the same of Welsh Cobs. Again, no hands went up. Then I asked, 'How many of you have heard of Shetlands?' Everybody including the smallest child shot their arm in the air! That laid the strategy for Myfanwy and I, when our sole income was to come from Ponies and Cobs that we had to make sure the whole world knows that the Welsh breeds are the most versatile in the world.

When Dyfed was little, people would come up to me and ask, 'So when are you going to buy him a Shetland pony?' Why would I want to do that?

Promotion, I believe, is the key to the continued success of the Welsh breeds. One exciting project we took part in back in 1979 was part of a BBC 2 *Diary of Britain* series called *Cob Country*. It followed the breeders, stud owners and enthusiasts around Ceredigion in the build-up to the Llanarth sale in the autumn. We were featured, with Sarah Hamer (née Edwards) of the Cascob Stud, who was a student with us then, John Roderick Rees with Rhosfarch Frenin, Dai Davies, Glanrannell, following his Cob Week participants, Pauline Taylor, Llanarth Stud and local veterinarian Tom Herbert. Of course many local 'celebrities' appeared on screen with several lively discussions including one on the topic of docking Cobs' tails. Miss Taylor and Tom Herbert were presenting a private members bill to have it banned. I was in favour of keeping it. I felt it was going against tradition and would spoil the look of the wonderful Cob back quarter. There was a purpose to docking in the days when the Cobs were working animals so that their tails didn't get entwined in the britching of the harness or collect mud from toiling in the fields. Now horses are mainly for leisure, so priorities have changed. The programme was greatly received and is still viewed on YouTube. The time is more than overdue for a repeat of that series from the BBC archives.

We were proud to take part in a great promotional event in Cardiff Castle in 1976, by invitation of the Benson and Hedges Show Jumping Championships. Twelve stallions were asked to parade over the three days to show the public the four sections of the Welsh Stud Book. I paraded 'Magic Bach' (Brynymor

Welsh Magic) alongside such greats as Coed Coch Bari and
Lyn Cwmcoed, to the delight of the crowd and the organisers,
Raymond Brooks-Ward and Tom Hudson. There was talk that
we would be invited to attend the London Olympia Show but
sadly this didn't materialise until 1984 when a display of Welsh
Cob stallions was choreographed by Jennie Loriston-Clarke. They
were shown, in-hand, driven and in a musical ride, culminating
in them jumping through hoops of fire. One of the lead horses
was Derwen Red Marvel, partnered by Hilary Legard so Derwen
was still, 'flying the flag'. I penned a poem for the occasion in
Cardiff:

> Benson and Hedges invited us down
> With Welsh Cobs and Ponies to Cardiff town.
> Jack Havard and Rosie and Rod came along,
> And Mrs Drew-Smythe was there in full song.
>
> Colin, Mostyn and Brian and Len,
> Gavin, the Hendys and Gareth came then.
> And Margaret in charge of her brother and dad,
> So therefore they couldn't do anything bad!
>
> Lyn and Norman, Cassino and Dafydd,
> Spritely and Golden, Michael, Meredith,
> Cardi and Magic, Spun Gold were in line,
> When John Cory said, come on Bari it's time.
>
> The caravan 'Ceulan' was so full of pop,
> And Ruth and her friend worked all day without stop,
> To tend to our thirst, and sell badges and ties
> And calm down Dr. Wynne with his loud, shrilling cries!

Col. Llewellyn invited us all
Down to the Angel to give us a ball.
The Baroness too saw to all of our needs,
And some drank so much, they went down on their knees!

John mawr Coed Coch was in fine voice that night,
But Harvey the V sign just wanted a fight.
But lucky for him that old Colin was cool,
Or otherwise he'd have been knocked off his stool!

At last it was over, the fun had to stop.
The stands were all silent, and so was the pop.
We'd battled that weekend through sunshine and wet,
But next year again boys, we'll be there I bet!

Just like when you are selling a car we have to be a step ahead of the competition and we have to take our produce to the customer. The quality of the product is vital and this can be controlled by educating people about the importance of selection when breeding. The big shows, like Lampeter and the Royal Welsh, propagate this selection process by rewarding the best animals. Trends change and tastes change in the showing and breeding world, certain types become more popular than others but whatever discrepancies appear they must be dominated by one thing and that is quality. As farmers have to produce good lambs with meat in the right quarter, so Welsh breeders must produce Ponies and Cobs that are attractive, have quality and do a job of work. That said, 'Beauty lies in the eyes of the beholder' – there is no such thing as the perfect type. Pentre Eiddwen Comet stood around 14.2 hh and Llwynog y Garth stood closer to 15hh, and they were two very different types, but two good Cobs. Comet was probably best described as stockier than Llwynog y Garth. But that is the great strength of the Cobs and indeed the Mountain Ponies; the difference and variety of types so that you can choose which you want yourself. Breeders such as Emrys Griffiths, The Revel, used a lot of Coed Coch blood in the make-up of his ponies. Criban Winston 1705 was by Coed Coch Glyndwr, and Revel Hailstone 1703 was also by Glyndwr, so you can see that those breeders saw the good in each other's animals even though they were fervent rivals in the show ring. When I look for a Mountain Pony I want to find a type of pony that I can put a child on his back and fly away.

I left a fortune in 1985. We had four garages in Aberaeron, Aberystwyth and Cardigan as well as the services in Llanrhystud, but one day I decided enough was enough and I left it all, in exchange for just the farm and the Cobs. My brother had a different philosophy to life, let's say. It's been hard work for Myfanwy and myself to re-start our lives down the line as it were, but I don't regret it for an instant, as we've been successful through hard work. Part of our success I do attribute to the fact that we were lucky enough to meet Gunn Johansson in 1986, as not only has she become a great friend but a tremendous supporter of the stud and the Welsh breeds. We were delighted that she was awarded an Honorary Life Membership of our Society.

Although the singing concerts, the cars and the cobs represented three different aspects of my life, they often overlapped. There was, for example, during recent years, a connection between the concerts and the cobs. Myfanwy and I decided to organise charity events to raise money for good causes by staging a Noson Lawen[2] at home.

As I was acquainted with so many stage and screen artistes throughout Wales we decided to organise these variety shows in the studs' main shed that is more of an arena. We began with a concert to raise money for the local community at Pennant. We succeed in raising £500, a goodly sum considering it was our very first venture.

We then became more ambitious and in 1994 we organised an open day with the proceeds going towards the Royal Welsh Show, specifically to the Cardiganshire Fund towards the Stables Appeal. This was followed by a Noson Lawen with some two dozen artistes appearing on the specially constructed stage. The programme was divided into four parts with a total of three dozen different acts. We held a raffle with one of the prizes being a painting by Aneurin Jones. We attracted an audience of more than 750 people to the shed and we raised over £8,000.

Unfortunately, during the evening's events the lights failed. The electricians present could find nothing wrong. Usually I am the least competent practical handyman in the whole of Wales but during this particular emergency I was the one who came to the rescue. I spotted a loose connection. The current was restored and the show restarted.

Electrical engineering has never been my forte. I once promised our resident students that I would supply them with a new colour television set. I bought one but back in those days sets were not already connected to plugs. Fixing the plug was the customer's

---

[2] A Noson Lawen is a traditional evening of entertainment with a variety of acts from comedians to soloists and choirs. They were traditionally held in country barns.

problem. I tried following the accompanying instructions but when I connected the plug to the socket and switched on there was no response on the screen. I took the set back to the shop in Aberystwyth, only to realise that I had mixed up the various wires! Since then, Myfanwy has been our emergency electrician.

Despite that early hiccup at our first great venture we persisted and organised another event towards raising money for the Royal Welsh the following year. It wasn't on such a grand scale but again we raised over £2,000.

In 2004 we organised a concert in aid of the Noah's Ark Charity Fund and raised £1,700 as well as over £1,200 for the Royal Welsh Centenary Fund. That same year I was invited to judge the Supreme championship in the horse section at the show, the highest honour I could ever hope to achieve.

In 2005 we organised a concert in aid of the Tsunami Appeal raising over £3,500. The following year we exhibited our Cobs and raised £1,200 towards Autism Wales. In all we have raised almost £20,000 for good causes.

Another of our ventures was named 'O Amgylch Swclod' ('Foaling Around'). This was staged in 2010 when Ceredigion was again the host county for the Royal Welsh Show. The President was Meirion, son of Aneurin Jones. Both father and son are artists of renown and the passing of Aneurin, late in 2017, was a sad day for Wales and the Welsh breeds.

We hope that we can continue to add to this total in small sums as and when we can. Health is everything. If you don't have your health you don't have anything. An old man once said to me, 'If you've got your health, you can do something about your problems!'

Life goes on. The mill wheel, if only allegorically, still turns. At the end of December 2013 I celebrated a big birthday. I reached the age of promise, 'oed yr addewid' as we say in Welsh. I received many birthday cards and wishes. I must refer to one in particular sent by my old friends John Gwynn and Olwen from Capel Seion, a card that included a Welsh poem written by Eleri Roberts. It went something like this:

Owner of the Derwen Stud, the singer Ifor Lloyd
Has reached his seventieth milestone, an age he can't avoid;
A winner at eisteddfods, at shows his cobs are best,
Today among his loved ones, he deserves a little rest.

His fondness for his noble cobs brings ardour to his breast,
Their fame both local and abroad surpasses all the rest;
Judging and showing horses are the pleasures he's enjoyed
As now today we raise our hats to breeder Ifor Lloyd.

The lure of retiring and moving to a nice little bungalow closer to town has never appealed. Never ever. Especially now that we've built and extended the farm over the years to how we want it. We've been here for 44 years so there's only one way I plan to leave! Dyfed is happily living in Swansea with Carly and our grandson Rhys Philip Ifor Lloyd, who must be the youngest ever member of the Welsh Pony and Cob Society. He was born at 5.00am and by 9.30am we were passing the offices in Bronaeron so I called in and made him a life member.

We plan ahead every day in the hope that the Derwen Stud of Welsh Cobs will continue for generations to come. I will end by paraphrasing a quote from the late Hannah Hauxwell, whose tough existence as a single farmer in the Yorkshire Dales was captured so poignantly in the documentary *Too Long a Winter*: 'Wherever I go, and whatever I do, this is, and always will be me.'

∾